Starting and Running a Business

on the
INTERNET

Alex Kiam and Tim Ireland

Contents

10 Very Good Reasons...

If you can answer "yes" to any of these questions then your business should be on-line....

1   Would your business benefit from being open 24 hours a day?

2   Are your competitors already on the Net or planning to go live soon?

3   Do you want to make money in a new and exciting way and establish your business as a forerunner in the biggest ever market place?

4   Do you send a lot of mail, faxes or make numerous phone calls?

5   Do you need to provide support for your products or services?

6   Do you currently utilise freephone telephone numbers or reply paid cards in direct mail?

7   Do you have any requirements for market research?

8   Do you need to send or receive large amounts of data such as graphics files to advertising agencies?

9   Can you afford the time necessary to set-up an Internet site and keep it dynamic?

10   Can you cope with the technical nature of the Internet?

Introduction

When it comes to business on the Internet, there is rarely a 'right' way - but there are plenty of wrong ways.

To the uninitiated, the concept of one-to-one relationships, the technology involved and the complicated online etiquette (Netiquette) can seem like a minefield. So the aim of this publication is to help you avoid the more common pitfalls and to come up with the right solution specific to your business.

In order to make this book as useful as possible, a dedicated web page has been created with links to resources mentioned in this book. So rather than searching around for the service or software mentioned, you can simply go along to the page (given below) and link directly to that which you require.

Furthermore, if the resource has moved, been discontinued or has simply changed its name, you'll find an updated link – again saving you time.

www.net-works.co.uk/run.htm

Chapter 1

Why should I be on the Internet?

Recent years have seen a headlong rush for businesses of all sizes to get on to the Internet. Many hundreds have done it properly and have seen their sales rise as a result. Many others have failed. The purpose of this publication is to give you the basics of how to get your business onto the Internet, ideally in a way that will make you money without over-spending, over-reaching or being ripped-off along the way.

Even though the commercial aspect of the Internet has only been evident for the last few years, large and small businesses from all over the world, in virtually every business sector and every business language, are already up and running. If you are NOT already on the Internet you can bet at least two of your competitors already are.

Yes, you will read conflicting views in various newspapers as to the profitability of the Internet, and whilst it is not disputed that some companies have yet to make a profit, being on the Internet now is akin to being 'in on the ground level'. Build your foundations now and the profits will come your way in the future.

There are far too many businesses and business sectors to cover in a publication of this size, but here are just a few examples of the types of businesses that are already making steady profits from the Internet.

Publishing

The Internet is a natural home for the publishers who are already familiar with presenting the printed word and graphics to unknown readers, so you will find that this is one business sector that has very few reservations about going live. If you look around, you will find a full selection of magazines, books and newspapers, all with their own Internet sites.

Publishers, like Net.Works at **www.net-works.co.uk**, have been quick to embrace all aspects of Internet trading.

Magazine publishing on the Internet, and on the World Wide Web in particular, has ballooned in recent years. Known as 'Ezines' they are amongst the most popular sites visited by the Internet users and cover a wide range of topics. For the most part, they are free to users and garner their profits from sponsorship of the site or the sale of related merchandise.

Mainstream publications with a strong print history tend to use a different technique. By providing a 'sneak preview' of their publication on a web site, they hope to stimulate interest in the latest (print) issue. Enabling subscription to the publication through the site also helps.

There are exceptions, of course. Two mainstream magazines that have certainly benefited from a dedicated Ezine are Playboy and Mayfair

- in fact, they constitute two of the most visited web sites of all time. Apart from increasing their printed paper circulation they are also receiving money directly by accepting advertising and selling Ezine memberships. Those memberships give subscribers access to particular parts of the web sites that casual browsers cannot reach. The reason why they are able to profit so readily in this way should be obvious, but we're going to try to avoid the subject of sex - at least until Chapter 6.

The 'sneak preview' technique is similar to an approach used by many book publishers. Instead of regularly updated pages, they tend to put up sample chapters of their new titles, using them to entice readers to buy the full product either directly through the Internet, or from bookshops. The International publisher, Penguin, is ranked amongst the best sites on the Internet for selling books. There are also some giant book retailers on the web, not the least being Amazon and BOL. You can also find smaller sites dedicated to one or two books often by self published authors.

It would be particularly remiss of us, as you'll read later, if we didn't take this *printed* opportunity to tell you about Net.Work's website at **www.net-works.co.uk** where you'll find details of our books, attractive discounts and a secure online ordering system.

Retailers

The benefit to retailers is obvious. Why put up with a shop in a back street of a small town when you can have a window to the world. By simply putting up your site on the Internet you are bound to get droppers in, and if you make your site interesting for them to visit you can bet that the word will spread round the Net and you will get even more visitors. Get it right and sooner or later the sales will start to appear.

Again, across the Net, you will find a wide variety of small and large retailers, from the largest supermarkets to little old ladies who sell bottles of the purest olive oil.

The beauty of the Internet is that the more individual your product, the more you can make out of a good Internet presence. As you are marketing to a much wider audience, your sales potential increases dramatically - especially if yours is a product that is hard to get, (or simply doesn't exist) elsewhere.

Goods which can be sold by mail-order find a natural home on the Internet.
CDnow delivers the music you want to your door very quickly and inexpensively.
Their site also offers album reviews, group biographies and tour information
which you are unlikely to find in a traditional music store. This site probably
represents the future of on-line shopping - no noisy crowds, no interfering
salespeople and a computer to help you search for the tracks you want!

http://cdnow.com/

Manufacturers

Although not selling direct to other Internet users, manufacturers have
still found the Internet an effective tool for doing business.

Once a potential business contact has been made, you can point
potential customers directly to your web site (rather than send out a
costly, soon-to-be out of date catalogue). Again, the more individual
your product, the more scope there is for your development on the web.

Those selling high value or technical products usually have to provide after-sales support to purchasers. Here, the Internet comes into it's own. You can upload the manual, a list of frequently asked questions, and extra information that comes to hand (such as patches to cover problems or bugs in software) to the Web. All the customer has to do is visit your website and browse through the info. After the expense of putting the details up there in the first place, there are no ongoing human resource costs. And if questions are still likely to arise, they can be dealt with by email, thus allowing your employee to deal with all queries in a 'batch' mode rather than destroying their working day through disruptive phone calls.

Apart from sales contacts and support, manufacturers have also found it useful for finding the right people for the job. Whether it be through direct advertising of vacancies, or by leaving a message in one of the many Newsgroups.

Contractors

So what if you've got nothing you can actually 'sell' over the Internet? More and more people are referring to the Internet to source a variety of services - and there are now many directories (like 'Scoot')

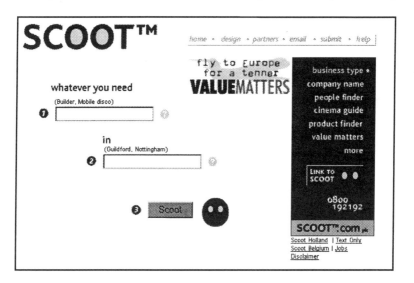

offering just this kind of search. If Yellow Pages offered you a free ad, would you turn it down? Of course, you wouldn't. Similarly, if there were a way you could have a brochure for next to nothing you would be mad to turn it down.

These are the primary benefits the web has to offer you. While an Internet user in Zimbabwe is unlikely to fly you in to fix his plumbing, a user more local who finds you in a directory - and better yet sees a web page outlining details of your services and credentials - is more than likely going to contact you first.

Consultancies

Very much in the same manner as manufacturers, consultants have found the Net an ideal place for making contacts and winning contracts. In some cases, a sample of work done in the past and published on the Internet has won lucrative orders. At the other end of the range, larger companies even offer free consultancy live over the network. It is amazing what answering a few email questions can do for your order book.

Business to Business

This is one of the most competitive areas of the Internet. Accountants, Lawyers, Bankers and even Estate Agents were at first slow to grasp the basics of the Internet. Initial attempts usually involved a simple presence featuring information about the firm, its services, clients and an enquiry service. Now there are firms of solicitors that offer (limited) free advice services over the web and huge search engines linking thousands of listings from hundreds of real estate agencies.

This kind of co-operation is a growing trend on the Internet. Similar businesses can gather together to give Internet users one place to look, thereby increasing the usefulness (and popularity) of the service and increase traffic for everyone involved. Collections of local businesses can get together to create a virtual 'business park', so anybody looking for a service in the local area knows where to look first.

> **Hint**
>
> If such a directory doesn't exist for your local town, opportunity knocks!

Chapter 2

The Internet - What it is, What it isn't, What it will be

Very
A \ Short History of the Internet
/\

Way back in the good old days of the cold war, some bright spark realised that once the bombs started to drop any central communications network would be less than likely to stay intact. This meant that their computers would not be able to exchange information, codes etc. - thus drastically reducing the opportunity to drop more bombs. What they created to combat this was a system that allowed their computers to connect to another via any remaining connections and transfer the information in 'packets'. In this way, the route the information took would be unimportant, as the information 'packets' could be reassembled at the other end regardless of how they got there.

Soon after, non-military organisations such as universities and research agencies got in on the act and started using the system to share information.

What really opened the system up, however, was the development of HTML (Hyper Text Mark-up Language). This allowed data from any source to be read by a number of different operating systems. The subsequent development of 'browsers' that could view such documents led to much wider use of this system of sharing information. In effect, anybody with a computer and connection could publish a text document on what was known as the World Wide Web.

By 1993, public use of this medium was increasing exponentially. The more people used it, the more it improved. The recent explosion in commercial interest has only served to open it up even more, to the point that getting online is now cheaper and easier than it has ever been.

Think of all of those wonderfully expensive television programmes that you get to watch absolutely free if you are willing to put up with a few ad breaks. It's the same principle at work, except in this case the medium allows you to produce a commercial of your own and make it available to millions for next to nothing.

Some Common Misconceptions

☒ **I have to stay connected to use email**

☑ You do not have to be online to read or write email, just to send or receive it. When someone sends you an email, it waits in a private box at your server until you connect to collect it - you then disconnect to read any mail you have received. You will not miss any emails because you are not connected when it is sent to you.

☒ **I have to stay connected for my web page to be live**

☑ You don't have to be connected to the Internet for your web pages to be 'live', as they are stored on your server and available to anyone who wishes to see them - 24 hours a day, seven days a week.

☒ **Someone viewing my web page has access to my computer**

☑ Only the information you have published to your web space is accessible to web users. There is no direct connection to your computer.

☒ **I need to learn HTML coding to build a web page**

☑ We're sure that there are many coders and programmers who would have you believe this. But in truth, there are many web authoring packages and tools that enable the average computer user to create a serious web presence from their desktop with only a passing knowledge of HTML.

☒ **150 million users = 150 million customers**

☑ It would not be true to say that you have access to 150 million users - in truth, it is the 150 million users who have access to *you* - and not all of them will be looking for, or interested in, what you have to sell. The trick is in targeting your potential customers and making sure that they find their way to your site.

☒ **There are millions of web pages - no one will be able to find me!**

☑ Nonsense. Again, it comes down to an understanding of how the web works. In fact, in this book we show you the quite simple measures you need to take to be found by those who are looking for your kind of business.

☒ **Advertising is unwelcome on the Internet**

☑ While it is true some of the more blatant methods of advertising are not tolerated in certain Internet communities, clever marketing is another matter entirely (this attitude is not particular to the web - think how popular unsolicited phone calls are). Soft sell is the order of the day, and if your page has content that represents value to the consumer, then all the better.

☒ **You can make lots of money overnight on the Internet**

☑ Oh, be reasonable. While the Internet does provide you with many new, exciting, (and often free) ways of promoting your business, it is not a magic cure-all. Like any business effort, it will require careful strategy, planning and lots of hard work.

☒ **The Internet is a waste of time and is unlikely to make you any money at all**

☑ This kind of reaction usually comes from those who have tried and failed - mostly because they have ignored or failed to grasp the individual marketing principles that apply to the Internet. For them, it's much easier to blame the Internet in general than accept the fact that they failed to understand the medium and/ or implement a successful business plan.

What the Internet Will Mean to Your Business

With good planning and a solid foundation, your Internet presence should become part of your regular promotional and sales schedule. It will not magically replace your need to promote your business in more traditional forms or lead to a million sales in the very first week, but carefully nurtured it will grow into a regular - and possibly even primary - facet of your business.

Chapter 3

How Much Will It Cost to Get Started?

It might actually be more fitting to ask, "How much will it cost me to ignore the Internet?"
If your competition is already utilising it, you stand a very real chance of losing a lot of business to them, due to an ever-increasing number of the population using various online directories and search engines to find what they are looking for. Still, you have this book in your hand, so you have taken that first important step of awareness.

That said, the cost of setting up a presence on the Internet varies from country to country (and from business to business). This chapter will give you an idea of those costs wherever possible, offer practical advice on how to minimise it, and show you how to avoid being ripped off.

Step 1 - Research

If you have no idea what the Internet is or how your competition is using it, then the first step will be research. This is the foundation of every successful business move.

The last thing you want to do is put your business straight on the Net if you are not ready to do so. If you make a hash of things in the very beginning, it is unlikely that you are going to be able to recoup all those potential customers who visited your site and decided that it was a waste of time. (If you have been in business for a while, then you will know how difficult it is to get rid of a bad name.)

> **Tip**
> Going straight to the support web page for this book at
> **www.net-works.co.uk/run.htm**
> is probably a good first step as there will be some handy research links there to get you started.

14

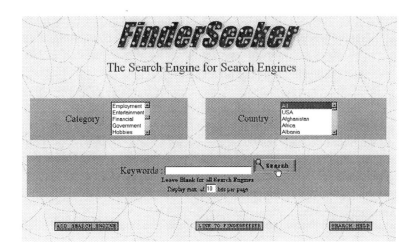

*Finderseeker helps you find topic-specific search engines
in a specified country*

www.finderseeker.com

If you already have a computer, the chances are that all you will need to invest in is a modem and Internet Service Provider (ISP). If you take it as read that your expansion to the Internet is inevitable, then it pays to make this minor investment sooner rather than later so you can conduct some serious research in your own time and at your own pace. (See the notes on Internet Service Providers in this chapter before you do this.)

If a more significant investment is necessary before you are 'Internet ready', then there are a number of more cost-effective ways to access the Internet for the purposes of research.

Here are a few suggestions:
- Local libraries and colleges often make Internet access available to the public. This may involve a small fee and times are usually limited to 30-60 minute windows.
- Net Cafes also offer Internet access by the hour - but it will cost you. Getting someone to show you how to use it costs even more. This is an option to be avoided if possible.

- If you have a friend with access to the Internet, ask if they can show you around. This is a most attractive option, as it is unlikely to cost you anything and you have someone you are familiar with to guide you through the basics.
- If all else fails - ask members of your family or staff. You may be surprised to find out who has been holding out on you (but more on that later).

When you do your research, it is probably best to take along a list of pre-prepared tasks to achieve, as it is **very easy** to be sidetracked when 'surfing'.

Among other things, you will probably want to know:
- What local business directories exist
- If there are any directories specific to your kind of business
- What local search engines are most popular
- If there are any search engines specific to your kind of business
- Who among your direct competitors is already online (take along a list of their names for keyword searches in the search engines and directories that you do find)

Step 2 - Gearing Up

Computer
The most obvious item required for access to the Internet is, of course, a computer. Depending on the situation you are currently in, you may have a few decisions to make.

I Already Own a PC
Congratulations, you are one step ahead. It is very possible that you will be able to get online immediately by investing in a modem and finding an ISP.

You should keep in mind, however, that once you get serious about the Internet you will need a computer that is up to speed. If your current computer is able to run Windows 98 - and has a fair amount of empty space on the hard drive - then you should be OK. After you have done some research and downloaded a little software you may find yourself

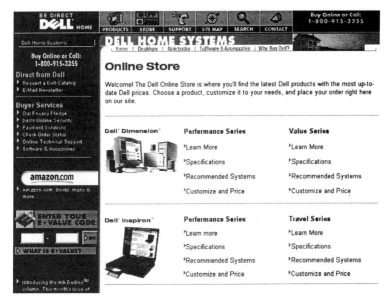

Design and build your own PC while online and get it delivered to your door

www.dell.com

wanting something more powerful, so you should start planning ahead for this. Who knows, you may even end up buying your new computer online.

I Already Own a Mac

Buy a PC. Sorry, I learnt on a Mac and have the greatest respect for them - but the fact remains that most of the free software available on the Internet (much of which you will be using to make your web pages) is for the PC. This alone is a good enough reason to make the switch.

Your business need not suffer from the changeover, as often it is a good idea for security reasons to ensure the computer you use for the Internet is 'isolated' and 'dedicated' - this means that you will be using it only to establish and regulate your web presence. You can continue to use your Mac as you always have to keep your accounts, type your letters and generally get on with business.

Also, the latest versions of Windows are very easy to adapt to. If you can use a Mac, then you will master Windows in next to no time.

Tip
'Package' deals from big-name retailers are for chumps. You will be paying through the nose for features you don't need and 'free' software you don't want.

I Don't Own a Computer

Buy a PC. Don't be swayed by price, opinion or flashy adverts for colour co-ordinated computers. You will need a PC to be able to take advantage of the huge range of free software that is available to help you make fantastic web pages without spending a penny.

What Should I Buy?

In essence you are going to need a PC that has been built in the last two years running Windows 98 or 2000, probably with a Pentium chip, at least 32 Mb of RAM and a suitable hard disk of over 1000 Megabytes (1 Gigabyte). A nice roomy hard drive is necessary to store the software you will be using to connect to your ISP, and to store any information or programs that you will be downloading from the Internet. Keep in mind that these specifications are the *minimum* that you will need to operate effectively.

Modem

A modem is a device that translates the data being sent or received over a telephone line. Because most people buying computers these days want it for access to the Internet, most new computers come with an internal modem as standard (this means that the modem is inside the 'tower', and you just have to plug a telephone line into the back of it). There are also stand-alone modems available, which can sit next to, or on, your computer.

Since all modems essentially do the same job, the only way of discerning between them is in terms of transfer speed -in other words how quickly can they translate your data into audio tones and audio tones back into data. That speed is measured in terms of baud (kilobytes of information per second - 'Kbps' or 'Kps').

If you are purchasing a modem complete with your computer, you may as well request one that runs at 56Kbps as this is at the higher end of what is available and is generally sold as standard.

Ensure that the modem you buy comes with all the necessary cables for connecting to your computer and the telephone line, and is approved by your local telecoms provider (it should have a sticker attached).

Telephone Lines

With modems getting as fast as they have been, generally there is no need to go beyond a standard phone line for Internet access.

Now you might be tempted to say; "Yes, I've already got a telephone line", but you must remember one thing. When you are on the Internet you are using your telephone line and anybody trying to call in will get the 'engaged' tone; therefore it is not recommended that you connect to the Internet using your day-to-day telephone number or telephone line. If your customers cannot get through, it is one certain way of losing business.

Instead you should either look towards getting a new line dedicated for Internet access, or as many small businesses prefer, use your fax line with a double socket connector.

Software

Mac or PC, the basic software that you require to access the Internet is usually provided free of charge by the ISP that you choose.

This software is comprised of a browser (that lets you 'surf' the web) and an email package (that lets you use email and Newsgroups).

Tip
Some telephone connections now allow for 'split' lines that will let you to make/accept calls and access the Internet at the same time. Ask your local telecoms provider to see if you are able to connect this way with your current service.

If you must connect to the Internet with a Mac then it is best to go with the latest version of 'Netscape Communicator' - purely because it comes with an extra web page editing ability that is probably your only 'free' option for this kind of software.

Otherwise, Microsoft Internet Explorer is the way to go - and is usually the standard software package provided by most ISPs (usually on a CD-Rom). As of going to print, the latest version of Explorer was 'IE5'. This also comes with a free web-editing package called FrontPage Express but you may also choose from dozens of others that are free to download for PC.

> ### Tip
> The latest versions of 'Word', the standard word-processing software for PC, come with great web-editing software that just about anybody can use. If you can use FrontPage Express, then you will be streets ahead with the latest Word package.

Internet Service Providers (ISPs)

Your Internet Service Provider performs a number of functions. Not only does it provide you with your connection to the Internet, but is also stores email that has been sent to you (until you connect to collect it), and more often than not provides web space for you to publish your own web pages.

This is the minimum level of service you are after, and these days you don't have to pay through the nose for it.

- Unlimited Access to the Web
- email account with 2-5 email addresses
- Access to Newsgroups
- 5-20 Mb of web space

You will also want to keep an eye on the following factors:

- **Local or Free Access Number -**
  Make sure the number you dial to access your ISP is a local rate or your phone bill will skyrocket overnight.

- **Customer Service -**
  Do they offer 'help' and 'how to' support to users? For instance, if you need help is this available only by email (not much use if you can't connect) or do they have a 24 hour 'helpline'? Also, how much information do they provide to help you add email addresses to your account, upload your web pages and so on. The large companies tend to be better for this kind of support, but often this is a 'timed' call that costs you money by the minute on premium rate.

- **Size** -
  Small companies may offer great deals, but will they be around in six months?
- **Reliability and Performance** -
  Again, the larger companies tend to be better as they have more hardware and can afford to run back-up staff and equipment. They do get busier at peak times, though.
- **Price** -
  This, you will agree, is the most important factor at the end of the day. There is a vast difference in cost for each part of the world, due mostly to market forces. The only golden rule is not to subscribe to a service which charges by the hour - this will nearly always cost you more in the end.

As you will see there are no right ways of joining the Internet but there are plenty of wrong ways. It is only by using the Internet and gaining more information that you are going to find the right service for you. Again, we come back to research.

If you do not make the right decision first time around, don't worry, as it is easy to switch between ISPs in the early stages of your Internet experience (i.e. before you set up a web site and print email addresses on all of your stationery). This is assuming of course, that you haven't paid for 6-12 months in advance - a very good reason to avoid this option if possible.

> **Tip**
> At www.net-works.co.uk /run.htm is a set of links to ISP directories for the UK, USA and Australia. Many of them offer comparative tables that should help you make an informed decision and this should be included in your initial research.

The biggest weapon you have in your armoury against being ripped off by an ISP is to increase your knowledge about the Internet.

Domain Names

A 'domain name' is the English language description of a set of numbers. Nobody, who has a life, is going to remember addresses that computers use to talk to one another. These are four sets of numbers from 0-255 separated by dots, known as IP addresses. Imaging putting on your stationery, "Please visit us at 215.45.2.91". The Domain Name simply translates the IP address into something like mydomain.com.

Now, because the computers use their own addressing system when talking to one another, we

A Happy Note

The harder it is for you to find your competitors on the web, the better things look for you. This usually means that they have not taken adequate steps to be found. With this publication you have a very real opportunity to achieve much better results.

humans are able to put any name to that set of numbers we like. So if you are given space on a computer known as 215.45.2.91 to other computers, you can call it what you like – unless, that is, someone else is calling their set of numbers by the same name. In other words, domain names have to be unique.

A decision on your domain name is a long way off at this stage of the discussion; in fact in the end you may even decide that you don't need one. If you make and list your web pages correctly, then having a domain name really isn't necessary.

You should also be aware that some ISPs (especially the 'free' ones) do not like you assigning domain names to your web space, but there are ways around this that we will outline later.

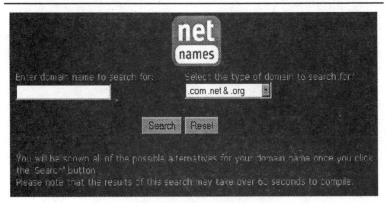

Find out if the name you want to use is free at
www.netnames.com

You will only really need a domain name if:

- You feel it is better for your corporate image
- You wish to print your URL (web address) on stationery, brochures etc.
- It is important to your marketing strategy (more on this later).

Domain names have two costs involved. One is the standard charge from the national registry for that domain (this is different for domain names ending in '.com', '.co.uk', '.com.au' and so on). The other is the charge from the company who is acting as the agent for the national registry. Agents charge ridiculously varying amounts for this, so again it is up to you to do a little research to avoid being ripped off. Visit www.net-works.co.uk/run.htm to link to one of the cheapest at present.

There is more information regarding this in Chapter 9.

The Building of a Web Site

This is another cost that can vary greatly, from the sweat of your brow to bills running up into the thousands. This publication shows you a number of ways to build your own web pages and publish them to the web space provided by your ISP.

If you DO wish to have your web page built by a third party, beware. There are several reasons why the Internet is referred to as 'the new frontier' - there are a lot of cowboys around, for one. If you are a relatively small business there shouldn't be any need for you to go to this expense. In fact, it's a fair bet that a friend, relative or staff member has already mastered the skill of building web pages, as it is very easy to learn. (See what we mean about people 'holding out on you'? You could very well discover that a younger member of your staff has a skill-set that you were completely unaware of.)

However it is also very hard to do properly, so before you commission anyone to build a web site for you, you should check out a few pages they have built.

A Happy Note

If you've designed a few brochures, posters, documents etc. in the past and they have been well received, then you will have no problems transferring these skills to the art of web page design.

Also, you should agree on exactly what you want for a set price.

Similarly, if you are wishing to build your own web site you should take a critical look at your own ability. In this book we will be showing you a great number of tips and tricks to make it easy to do, but in the end the 'look' of the page is up to your own design skills and eye for beauty. (It would be very much the same if you were taught how to paint. How you applied those skills, and the end result, would depend a lot on your innate artistic ability.)

Maintenance

Independent experts have calculated that the cost of your system and connection charges will only account for around about 20% of your total cost of setting up your web site. Training and personnel costs, site maintenance and/or the labour costs of dealing with Internet enquiries usually take up the remaining 80%.

This isn't as scary as it sounds, as you can minimise these costs with some smart management and by following the tips in this book. For instance, if you were to train a member of your staff to maintain a site it would probably be a good idea to start with a junior member. They are not only quicker to pick it up; they are more cost effective in terms of wage and will appreciate the opportunity to advance.

Net Sushi specialise in designing simple commercial websites - these are often better received by the customer than flashy, expensive multi-media sites

www.net-sushi.com

Chapter 4

Email = Free Mail

How would you like to mail all of your customers and potential customers and have them receive your brochure within minutes - even if they live on the other side of the globe - for the price of a local phone call? How would you like to be able to send a detailed report - including any relevant documents or files - to a friend or colleague in seconds, without so much as a staple or an envelope?

Just a couple of small examples of what email is capable of - and why it is the most used application on the Internet.

It's your route to the highest savings, a good profile, and instant return on your investment on joining the Internet. Indeed it is a reason for joining the Internet all on its own. Anybody who has discovered the time and cost advantages of sending faxes instead of ordinary mail will positively love email.

It's no wonder that those who have already been converted to the world of email refer to the normal system as "snail mail". Used properly, an email system is just like having an internal phone network within your business, but extended all round the world.

Cost Savings

Almost the entire cost of an email system is in the set up. Once you have got your computer, modem and access provider sorted, you will find it is almost as cheap to send thousands of messages as it is to send just one.

The two most obvious savings are in the cost of printing onto paper - either from your desktop or through a professional printer - and the savings on standard mailing charges or long distance phone calls.

Anybody who is familiar with direct mailing or who has sent out brochures to their customers will realise that a half to two-thirds of the costs involved is the price of the mailing piece and the postage to its

Sending an email

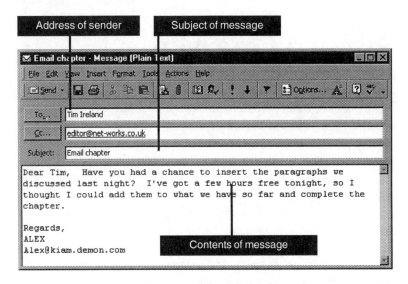

Sending an email Notice the option to copy the message to other people. If you don't want the recipient to know you have sent copies to someone else, use BCC instead of CC!

required destination. Here the benefits of sending an electronic signal to almost anywhere in the world on the same day are obvious. It makes testing and advertising a whole lot cheaper, thus making the marketing and development of new projects that bit more viable. By removing the overheads you can either get projects off the ground that would never have happened, or you can increase your profits on those that would have added to the bottom line anyway.

You will also find the environmental considerations of not having so much paper floating around provides cash benefits. No longer will you need boxes and files to store your received orders for the last six years. Never again will you have to retype an incoming message or letter (as when you 'reply' to an email, it includes all of the text within the message you are replying to).

Receiving an email

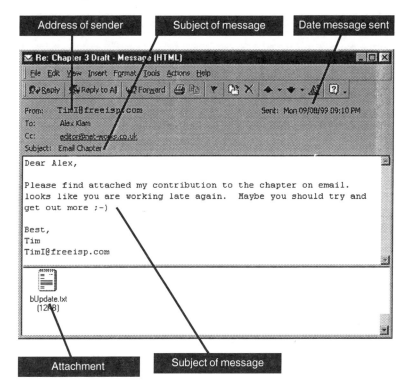

Receiving an Email: *The ease of filing, deleting, forwarding or replying probably explains why more Email is read and dealt with than normal mail items.*

Case Study

Here at Net.Works we often exchange documents, research and sometimes entire publications with associated publishing companies in the US and Australia. In fact, when the original text for this book was finished, it was forwarded by the Authors to the main publishing office as an email attachment (along with some picture references for the graphics department).

Filing and managing your email

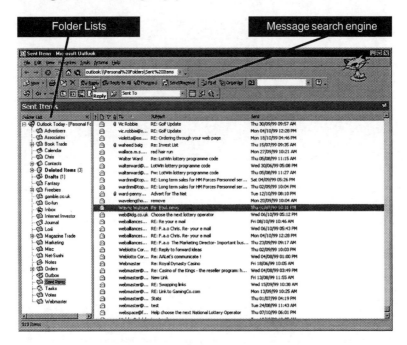

Microsoft Outlook provides many ways of filing and managing your personal and business emails - there's even a powerful search engine built in!

In the old days (that's before 1994!), the cost, in time and materials, of having copies of relevant documents made, packing them up and posting them or using a courier down to Australia was immense. But since joining the Internet, we've been able to reduce those costs to roughly 1% of the previous bill (yes, one percent!).

As a recent example, an entire manuscript was loaded onto the Internet from Australia and sent directly to us in the UK. Once downloaded it was only a matter of hours before the document had been edited, typeset and made ready for the printers. Then, just as it was about to go, we discovered a file was missing.

Normally this would have been a disaster. It would have meant frantic phone calls in the middle of the night, a delay of a couple of days while the files were sent by international courier, other delays as they were cleared through customs, and a third delay as they were retyped or loaded onto our own computers.

However we were able to send an email which alerted our Antipodean friends by an audible beep on their computer. The necessary file was back in our offices within five minutes flat. A significant delay had been avoided - as had downtime charges at our printers - and none of our customers were aware of the mad panic that had gone into creating their publication.

Service

The speed with which you will be able to deal with your existing and new Internet customers will show through as an improvement in your service. The response to requests will be almost immediate and it's bound to impress, especially in time sensitive situations.

There will be no more delays while you wait for your brochures and other documents to appear from the printers. There will be no more delays as you try to reach somebody by phone and there will be no more delays when you miss that last postal collection. It is convenient for you, it's convenient for your staff and it's convenient for your customers.

Have you ever promised to respond to a customer immediately, done all of the hard work and then found it impossible to contact them by phone? Well, sending an email will remove your worries. Gone are the days of the busy signal and the endless waiting on hold, by sending an email you can make sure that your message reaches its destination whether the recipient is in or not. The moment they get back to their desk they will see it.

If you are trying to contact somebody who is being particularly elusive, you will no longer have to put up with the excuse from a secretary that he has gone out, is having her hair done, or is just not available. You can send an email message and shortcut all those blocking techniques.

Other positive service gains include the sending of newsletters to all of your customers to keep them up to date with the latest goings-on within your business. You can even customise them before they go out to make sure that they are not discarded. With the process being almost immediate, it is like sending out a continuous stream of press releases.

Finally, the simple act of putting an email address on your business cards and letterheads is like giving your existing customers and potential customers a freephone telephone number. If they are on the Internet or have access to an email system, it is also virtually free for them to send mail to you.

Added Bonuses

Apart from the cost savings and improved service that you can give through email, there are many major added bonuses. Perhaps at the top of the list is the fact that most people read their email messages as opposed to throwing them in the bin or simply not answering the phone. They find it easier just to click open a file and see the basic information, than they do to open a letter and sift through the various pages inside to understand what it is all about.

Your email messages will also be easier to send on to other parties. For example, if you send an email to the wrong department within a company, it can be redirected in seconds (rather than lie in somebody's in-tray until they get around to dropping back to the mail room). Similarly, if someone wishes to forward your mail (or even just some relevant comments) to another party, it can be done quickly, quietly and correctly at the click of a button.

A big plus for you and your customers is the ease in which you can reply to an email. Having read an incoming message on your screen you can format the reply within your head and type it onto your machine within seconds. Just a click of your mouse can have it transmitted back to the person who sent you the original message without even having to type their address. It is so easy that you will find the backlog that normally builds up in your in-tray a thing of the past. As you well know, not a lot of work gets done once the in-box overflows into the 'too hard' basket - and email makes it much easier to deal with matters immediately.

Dealing with an email is also easier than dealing with an incoming phone call (even though the response time can be just as immediate).

For a start, you don't have to 'think on your feet' quite so much - and we all know how tricky this can be when dealing with complaints or discussing price.

Instead of having to come up with a reply instantly, (acting hastily and possibly making a mistake, or making an offer of a discount without doing your calculations) you can take your time over composing an email message. By using up just a fraction of the time you saved over traditional methods of sending a reply, you can make yourself sound more eloquent, cover all of the necessary points and be sure of your facts before you send it off. The days of putting down the phone and thinking "damn" could be gone for ever.

Two other bonuses of sending email, are that you will always know where it has come from and that undelivered mail will be returned to you. The header on incoming messages will not only tell you who sent the message in the first place, but it will also tell you the route that it took to reach your computer. It can be especially useful in understanding the structure of the organisation you are trying to deal with.

Undelivered mail will also generate an electronic message that will immediately come back and tell you about it. If the email address you have got is wrong, their account has been closed, or they have moved to a different site you will be instantly notified and you can amend your mailing list accordingly. It is most unlike the traditional mailing system where a returned package can often disappear in the black hole of the Belfast Sorting Office, for weeks if not months on end, and all the while you are sending out more expensively printed, stamped and packaged mailings to the same address.

Mailing Lists

While it's easy to say that you can send thousands of emails in one press of a button, there are a few practicalities to consider. Of course, you will need to keep the email addresses of the people who you wish to send messages to. Most standard email packages available can easily handle 400 to 500 different names and let you arrange them into groups, but if you want more you will probably have to get some proprietary software created, or purchase one of the specialist commercial packages available.

Alternatively, there are also sites that offer free 'list servers' to help you further automate subscription to your mailing list.

Once up and running your mailing list server will be so easy to use that you will be tempted to mail all of your prospects continually. Naturally, this would be a disaster so you will have to exercise a bit of restraint and use some common sense when playing with your new toy.

You will also need to obey the usual rules as if you were dealing with a standard mailing list. For example, if somebody wishes for his or her name to be removed from the list, you should make sure that you do it immediately. So, you will need to make sure that your list is cleaned regularly removing redundant entries, and any errors that may creep in. But if your normal business includes sending direct mail, then stick to the normal maintenance procedures and it should prove no problem at all.

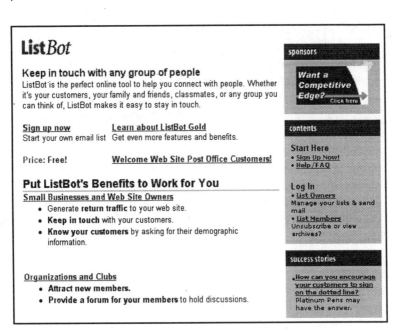

Start your own email list at

www.listbot.com

You will find that the scope for personalising mailing shots using mailing list software and the email system is immense. You can look forward to letting your computer do all the hard work in searching out the part of your brochures, price lists and product updates that only a particular group of clients would be interested in. This should see an end to the term 'junk mail' since no longer will the recipient receive the 'junk' part of a mailing. They will only see the parts that are relevant to them and will enable them to make a quicker response. You might even find your customers sending a reply email thanking you for keeping them up to date so quickly and so regularly.

Newsgroups

Despite the name, Newsgroups have little to do with news. They are, in effect, electronic noticeboards where you can post an announcement, pose a question, or reply to a posted question with an answer.

It is in Newsgroups that you have the best chance of targeting a particular group based on an individual interest, profession or location (and as there are tens of thousands of Newsgroups, it is more than likely that you will find one or two that will be useful to you).

HOWEVER, (and here's the catch) you must remember that Newsgroups are communities of people that jealously guard the integrity of their group and the subject that they wish to discuss. Posting a message that is 'off-topic' or a blatant advertisement is widely frowned upon - and often banned outright. Doing this would make you about as welcome as a door-to-door salesman at a cocktail party.

The best way to promote your business via a newsgroup is participate in the discussion. Generally, a link to your web site is tolerated as part of your signature at the end of the message. If you participate in the group in an intelligent, friendly and helpful manner, then there will be many that will wish to see your site of their own accord.

Important - Be aware that while you participate in a discussion you are an ambassador for your company. If you say anything belligerent or inappropriate, it will reflect badly on your business and is unlikely to be forgotten in a hurry.

A Few Warnings

As you will be aware, the Internet is not entirely secure. It is possible to intercept and read emails. However intercepting a message requires a high level of technical ability. It also requires some pretty snazzy software. There is little chance of just a casual browser ever seeing what is in your private emails. However, if you do have to send some sensitive information, and fear that somebody may be deliberately trying to read your email, there are professional 'encryption' packages available that jumble the messages before they go and decipher them at the other end.

The Internet also suffers from a small amount of reliability problems. Not all emails that are sent, arrive. Although the percentage is very small, it does happen. However, just think how many ordinary mail messages go missing and how many times you have been cut off while trying to make a phone call. In the scope of things, the Internet is no less reliable than snail mail or the standard telephone and, in fact, most studies seem to show that it is more reliable than the traditional methods.

Since sending an email is so easy you will find that you will probably receive a lot of messages from Day One of being connected on the Internet. It is important that you do not allow a huge backlog to develop and that you do not simply dump all the mail you receive in your in-box. Very soon you will not be able to find that important message you received about two weeks ago. So make sure that you create an adequate filing/folder system and use it efficiently, just as you would with your standard mail.

Tip
Flaming

You have been flamed when you have received an angry email message, often full of abuse and obscenities. Be careful how you deal with these and NEVER ever flame back. The last thing you want is someone working as hard as they can to ruin your business. They have access to the same wide audience as you do and probably have more time on their hands to indulge in such childish activities.

Also, if you run a large organisation, do not forget that you will have to assign somebody the job of dealing with incoming email (unless you are willing to deal with it yourself). Not only will they need to be trained in how to send and receive email, but you will have to teach them how to clean the existing email lists and take out any mistakes. You may also want the same person to deal with your Internet access provider and web site maintenance. And, don't forget to make plans for that employee's absence.

You will also find yourself getting a lot of junk mail, otherwise known as 'Spam'. Delete it and ignore it - you cannot avoid it and 'fighting back' is always more trouble than it is worth.

Similarly, you may be tempted yourself to send an unsolicited email to hundreds of people at once. Unlike a mailing list, (where you are dealing with voluntary participants) this kind of promotion is heavily frowned upon by web users and will only result in derision and heartache. Don't do it.

Most current email programs come complete with a 'spell-checker' that checks every email before it is sent. Use it. You will find that your spelling suffers a lot when writing email - and someone reading an email touting your 'professional' services is unlikely to be impressed.

Our final warning centres on the ease with which you can read, type and send email. This, combined with the anonymous interface you are dealing with, often leads to messages that are erroneous, belligerent, or otherwise regrettable. Don't forget that an electronic message is just as permanent as a printed page. If you let off steam or send a hastily created message and later regret it, you will find that your boob could echo around the Internet for an unexpectedly long time. This is quite a common problem relating to email, and is very similar to the change in personality that occurs when you get behind the wheel of a car.

Chapter 5

Don't Ignore Your Browser!

While email may be the most-used tool on the Internet, it must be said that web pages are by far the most useful - and the most versatile. Yes, there is a lot of junk out there, but once you know where to look you will find that the World Wide Web is a great resource that can save you a lot of time and money.

You should make a habit of using the web wherever possible. It may seem rough going at first, but once you get into the swing of things you will find yourself turning to the web more and more for answers. Besides, if you plan on building a web page yourself it is important that you have a clear idea as to how others go about it. You will also find yourself developing a better understanding of web users psyche along the way.

Everyday Uses

The web is many things to many people, but in its main practical sense it is the world's biggest library. On it you can find encyclopaedias, dictionaries, maps, plus information and articles covering just about every subject you can imagine.

There are also a variety of regional tools and directories that can give you instant updates regarding the weather in Sydney, the time in California, the current value of the Dow Jones Index and the latest news headlines.

There are even tools that let you translate text from English to a number of languages and vice-versa. If you can name a practical application, it's a fair bet that it exists somewhere on the Internet (and if it doesn't, opportunity knocks yet again).

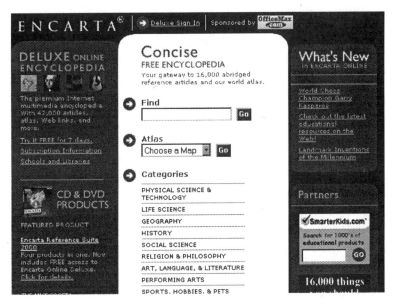

You'd be amazed how much information that can be found for free on the web which you would normally expect to pay for.

Market Research

The Internet really is a market researcher's dream. On it are millions of sources covering just about every subject you could imagine. Finding what you are looking for is as easy as typing the relevant words into a search engine.

The nature and depth of your research will depend largely on the nature of your business and the way you normally conduct it. If you are a local plumber it may be as simple as using search engines to find out which of your competitors are on the Internet and where they are listed. If your needs are more complex than this or if you live for statistics and feedback, then you will be happy to know that detailed market research on the Internet is far easier than in the 'offline' world. Chances are someone has already done research that suits your needs and published it - and if not you can simply find the right newsgroup and ask.

Once you have an Internet connection and your web site is up and running, your market research becomes even easier (see Chapter 12).

Shopping

Yes, shopping. On the Internet you can not only buy computers and software, but also electrical goods, furniture, office supplies, vehicles, real estate, airline tickets - and sometimes even lunch!

If you run a small business, you've probably had problems in the past finding the time to hunt down the best price. The Internet not only makes it easier to find local retailers and wholesalers, it also makes it much easier to compare their prices and/or services. If you don't like what you see, another store is just a few clicks away. Even better, if you can't find what you're looking for locally you can now order it from overseas with the click of a button.

Finding It

The Internet is a big place, but for the most part you can just go to your search engine of choice and enter a few related words (known as 'keywords') to find what you're looking for. Yes, often it is that easy.

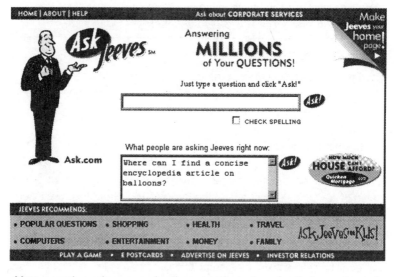

Meta search engines search other search engines for their results and then compile them into one list

www.askjeeves.com

Yahoo is still the most popular search engine on the Net

www.yahoo.com

Apart from a list of the most useful search engines, the *Starting and Running a Business on the Internet* web page also features some local tools and directories for your area and a great place to start.

Finding it Again

Once you find something particularly useful, you should save a link to that page in your 'Favorites' (these are also known as 'Bookmarks'). You should not only get in the habit of doing this wherever possible, but also keep your 'Favorites' organised in a system of folders (like 'Local', 'Research', 'Shopping' and so on).

Most browsers will also let you save a choice selection of 'Favorites' to a special toolbar so they are only one click away. Because their browser often comes with some links already installed here, (mostly for promotional purposes) many people are afraid to change them. Don't be. You should add sites you use most often to this toolbar.

Similarly, you should also change the default 'home page' (the page that appears when you first connect to the Internet) to something more immediately useful if you see fit. This is easy enough to change in the 'Options' or 'Preferences' of your browser,

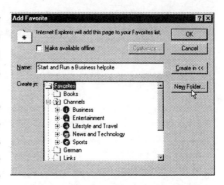

To save searching for your favourite sites every time you log on, add them to your "favourites"

and can be anything from a particularly useful search engine to, once it is live, your own web site.

Learning by Doing

Along the way you will find pages that look stunning and pages that look stunted. Some places will be easy to find and others you will simply stumble across when you least expect it. All of this should be an ongoing learning process for you, as you find out more and more about what measures these sites have taken to be found, and what they do to keep your attention once you arrive.

With this in mind, don't be afraid to check out the occasional distraction. If anything catches your eye, click through to see it. Important lessons can be learned by seeing how others do this and what they have to offer when the user clicks through.

After all, the big secret to having a well-travelled page is knowing how to be found - not only by those who may be actively looking for you, but those who need your kind of business and just don't know it yet.

You will end up on many sites that have a particularly useful tool, informative content or sometimes just an entertaining angle. Sometimes this has a direct link to the type of business they run (like FT.com having a share price index, for instance) while others will simply have something that, however unrelated, gets attention.

Chapter 6

Capturing the Imagination, Delivering the Goods

Just as you would not place a printed page on the television, or hold up some toothpaste and smile brightly for a radio commercial, so you should not expect your existing techniques to work on the Internet.

Instead, you need to treat the Internet as a completely new media. As we discussed in the previous chapter, you need to get out there not only to discover how it works, but you will probably need to spend quite bit of time online to fully understand who inhabits this electronic world. Without hands-on experience, you cannot possibly get into the minds of web users and understand what makes them tick. As you know, until you fully understand the market you cannot hope to make your sales.

What you will discover, and probably start to feel for yourself, is that when getting online most users are after:

- Useful Information
- Something Free
- Entertainment

Or, failing that:

- Sex

We'll ignore sex, (just for the moment*) and focus on the first three to see how you can best get people to your site of their own volition. What we're talking about here, quite frankly, is bait - but keep in mind that if, once they arrive, users are unhappy with what they see they will be off the hook in a flash.

If you really can't wait, try reading **Sex on the Internet, also published by Net.Works ;-)*

The trick is offering something of value and delivering it, (or something of equal or greater value) once the user arrives at your site.

Now, if you're a consultant who is paid for advice or writes articles or reports of value, then a decision on your bait is quite straightforward. As you have a specific corner of the market to target, you need to look out there and see what else is available. If it's a little thin on the ground, then you can immediately benefit by publishing excerpts from your articles to get people to your web page and interested in your services. If there's material just like it all over the web, you'll have to take things a step further. Read on.

If you offer a common service like plumbing, then your focus is primarily on locale. Obviously you can't travel to Mauritius to fix a sink (though it would be nice). Your main bait therefore would be a service of use to the local community, like a local trade directory for your town. Of course, some tips on your site about how to make emergency repairs before you arrive would also be appreciated. Capture and delivery.

If you sell something that can be shipped worldwide, (or even transmitted by email) then the world is your oyster. If you have a specialised service or product that is rare, then your content is educational background about that service or product or a closely related topic. Again, have a look on the web to see what is out there and fill in the gaps. Say, for instance, you make pure leather shoes, a good idea for your bait would be helpful information for the millions out there who are allergic to rubber and/or rubber adhesives.

Unfortunately, if you are targeting the world market with a common product or service, then you will really need to put your imagination to work. This is where entertainment and, most importantly, a sense of humour come into play. Try to get into the minds of your potential customers, then go lateral. For instance, there's a Canadian company that sells maple syrup. At first glance, their hilarious page appears to be about Canada's bid for world domination. From the options given on the page, one in particular stands out - that for recipes (which, of course, involve a certain brand of maple syrup that you can buy through their site). Again, the imagination is captured and two desirable qualities, (useful information and entertainment) are delivered.

The angle or theme you take with this kind of approach doesn't have to have a strong link to the kind of services you provide, but it can help if it is a showcase for your talents. Web Designers and writers, for example, can produce bait on just about any theme they choose to tout their services - and on this note, finally, we come to sex.

If you've been through a few searches before, you will have noticed that completely unrelated pornographic sites sometimes end up among your results. This is because promoters of these sites often produce huge pages full of text in the hope that, when it does turn up in an unrelated search, the user will think 'oh, what the hell' and check it out. (This is an extremely annoying practice, but you must admit that they are on to a fairly good bet. After all, how many products are as widely popular as sex?)

A certain writer, who shall remain nameless, decided to turn the tables on this highly unpopular technique by creating a page that openly touted a 'pornographic' site based on some very popular keywords at the time. These keywords were, (in no particular order) 'Gillian', 'blow', 'Anderson', and 'job'. When arriving at this page the user saw an open parody of a porn site (sans nudity, of course) - and an animation of Gillian Anderson's head exploding. Don't laugh. The site received upwards of 3,500 hits a week for over six months with no promotion whatsoever, apart from a

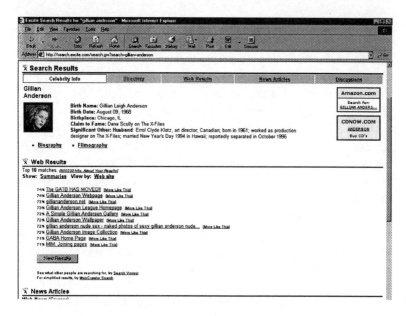

A search for Gillian Anderson will produce everything from biographical details and fan-club sites through to computer wallpaper and, of course, a clutch of sex sites

listing in five - yes, only five - major search engines. Over 10% of users clicked through to the main site resulting in at least one enquiry a week for projects that, unsurprisingly, involved humour and/or web site promotion.

Again, capture and delivery - this time, capture on the basis of sex and delivery of entertainment.

Now we've got the sordid business of sex out of the way, the rest is up to you. The successful promotion of your business needs to be something that:

- Does not currently exist on the web
- Is likely to be sought after by your targeted market
- Offers something of value

If you know what that is, you're ready to take the next step.

Chapter 7

The Big Decision

Interest in the World Wide Web is growing at a phenomenal rate. It is by far the fastest growing area of the Internet today. It is easy to understand, simple to use, and even non-technical people use it and feel at home with it. Simplicity of use is the key; to move around you simply see something of interest, point your mouse at it, and click. With the World Wide Web your terminal turns into a form of TV controller where the button you press determines what you will see - and the analogy with television does not end there.

The World Wide Web makes cruising the information super-highway a form of entertainment. But it is entertainment with a difference. The interactivity and the feeling of doing something can heighten the experience of Internet surfers. By providing an outlet for these energies, say by making a sale, or providing a service, you can bring a form of gratification to visitors of your web site, which will cause them to return and create future sales.

To many people, the World Wide Web **is** the Internet. However, many people thought that of Gopher until it was superseded. In this world of rapidly changing technology who knows what will happen next?

Why is the web so attractive? There are many subtle reasons, but three stand out head and shoulders above the rest - graphics, constant change, and hypertext links (instant links to relevant information on your site or another on the World Wide Web). The graphics add life to otherwise tedious text files; the ability to change the web site so often provides for ongoing "entertainment", and hypertext links provide a way of jumping around the Internet or contacting you with the click of a button. This saves the casual user the effort of looking up an address for other interesting sites, it removes the need to memorise otherwise unmemorable strings of text, and the sense of not always knowing where you are going provides for more entertainment (known as surfing).

As well as being a reason to surf the Internet, these three reasons provide a benefit for you as a business. They allow you to make your presence more interesting and it keeps the information you are giving up to date. Take the simple example of perhaps your most used tool, the catalogue. Imagine that you have just finished a large print run for your latest annual catalogue and before the ink is dry on the paper you notice an important typo. You have the option of sending out the error included with all the embarrassment that will bring, or the alternative of an expensive reprint. Then, days after it has gone out, you acquire an important new product. Sure you can send out a separate flier or update with all the expense entailed, but it is not quite the same as having that product in your original catalogue. Nevertheless, you struggle through and your customers have now received your catalogue with typos and an update flier. It is just then that your suppliers decide to increase their charges. Do you go for another reprint, another update, or reduce your margin? In the Internet world, none of these complications are real problems. That is because your World Wide Web page can be updated within minutes of any changes being identified. What is more, those necessary alterations can be made for next to no cost.

On top of the cost and time savings of being able to continuously update your information, you will have the added benefit of there being virtually no limit on the amount of detail you can offer your customers. Where printing charges and mailing costs may have limited the scope of your real world brochure, the World Wide Web offers no such limitations. That is because you do not have to be worried about confronting your prospective customer with information. The judicious use of different pages, of hypertext links and anchors, will allow browsers of your site to self-select the sections that affect or interest them. And now, with the customer being in charge, you can use software to completely automate any transactions that are made. So, in effect, the World Wide Web allows you to create a retail outlet that covers the globe, is open 24 hours a day for 365 days a year, and which contains no staff. Is there a better way of increasing sales per employee?

If you need any more reasons why you should put your business on the web look no further than the information you will receive back. The details you can automatically capture, and those you can get your prospects to send you, will allow you to learn more about your customers. That information can then be used to make changes to your web pages to make them more interesting to your specific customers. This constant feedback of real time information will allow you to measure the effects and benefits of any changes that you make to your site. So you will know the results of any testing that you implement almost immediately, and you can use these to update your site to meet your customers' precise requirements.

As you can see, there are many reasons why a web site makes good business sense. By now you probably even have your concept for a World Wide Web page, but who is going to create the different pieces? You and other members of your company are the cheapest option. But do

It would not be financially viable for Net.Works to produce a printed catalgue with this amount of detail for each of its books. But on the Internet you can put as much information as may be needed by your customers.

Also, a new book can be added to the online catalogue in minutes. If an existing book goes out-of-print, it is simply removed. price changes can also be easily accomodated.

you have the necessary skills or the spare time to acquire those skills, and can you do it in time to meet any deadlines?

Perhaps the best approach is to initially use others' expertise to create your web location and then learn as you go along, so that in the long run you can do it all yourself.

If you already use a traditional advertising agency do not automatically turn to them to help you out on the Net. This is one area where expertise and technical knowledge is more important than the ability to visualise a selling message. Try asking a few basic questions such as which servers they are familiar with, for how long they have been writing HTML, and for their opinions on using Flash. Unless you get an instantaneous and comprehensive answer (and if they even joke about washing powder), try looking elsewhere - or consider doing it yourself.

Even if you are settled on the idea of hiring professional help, we suggest that you read the following few chapters regardless as at the very least it will make you a more informed consumer. Big or small, the principles remain the same (and you would be surprised at how many 'professional' services do not include vital services like professional copywriting or the inclusion of an effective search engine strategy).

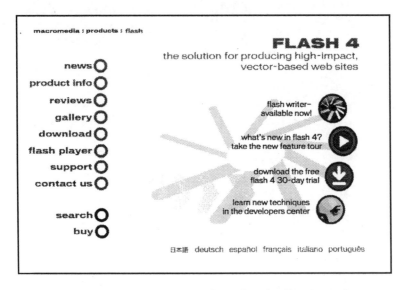

Does your agency know its Flash from its Shockwave?

Chapter 8

Domain Names and Hosting

Domain Names - a Snappy Address

Domain names are useful to a point, and can give a more 'corporate' image - but are not always necessary. If you wish to print your URL (web site address) and/or email address on stationery, then you may well prefer something like **www.businessname.com** and name@businessname.com to **www.servername.com/~business/** and businessname@businessname.servername.com.

Also, if you have a distinctive and well-known brand name or an individual product, then there will be a lot of people who, before they go to a search engine, will take a punt on www.yourname.com.

The cost varies greatly, so if you do wish to have one it pays to shop around. Remember that once you settle on a domain name it is yours 'forever', (renewable every two years) so if you change servers it will have no impact on your URL or email addresses.

Sometimes a deal with a certain ISP or 'Virtual Server' (someone who hosts your web page and redirects your mail, but has nothing to do with your everyday connection to the web) involves a 'free' domain name. These may look like a good deal - but read the fine print carefully to see if moving to another ISP or Virtual server involves surrendering your domain name or paying a substantial fee.

For the most part, a web site for a small business will not need a domain name. If the right description and keywords are chosen, you will be found.

If Someone Already Owns a Domain Name with Your Name

Often the same brand name is registered in different countries, and as .com is (un)officially a US domain, (and where the web first took off) the chances of getting **www.yourbrand.com** are usually slim. Also, there are people out there who are buying up domain names in the hope that they will be bought by someone desperate for it.

If **www.yourbrand.com** is taken, you can also try alternative domains like **www.yourbrand.net** or even regional ones like **www.yourbrand.co.uk** (United Kingdom) or **www.yourbrand.com.au** (Australia).

The other alternative is to set up a site with a domain name that has nothing to do with your current brand name or product. What, for example, does the Amazon have to do with books? Why is a web design company called Net Sushi? And, if you didn't already know, could you guess what eBay do?

Choosing a Non-Branded Domain name

Clarity Communications, a highly respected advertising and web design company in the UK, has very cleverly chosen the domain name **www.marketing.com**, knowing full well that the occasional managing director will end up on their site purely by chance.

Similarly, Roto-Rooter, (a popular and well-known pipe-cleaning company in the US) have not only registered **www.rotorooter.com** but also **www.plumber.com** to ensure that they are found by the people that need them.

We have also talked about how common 'typos' are when using search engines, and users typing well-known domain names are prone to similar errors. An enterprising chap recently took out the domain name www.infaseek.com for this very reason and as a result gets a lot of visitors to his trading site. You may also be surprised to find yourself at a sex-related site when you spell Guinness with one 'n'!

Again, it is up to your judgement to choose an appropriate domain name. Have a look, find out what's available and get creative.

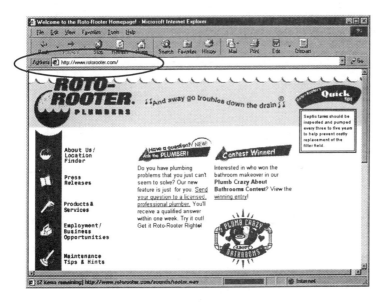

Spot the Difference
Rotorooter benefits from hits via a branded and non-branded domain name

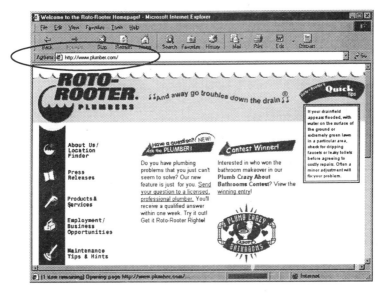

Servers - Where Your Web Page is Stored

You have three basic choices of where to put your site. You can create and run your web site on your own equipment, you can use an ISP, or you can use a "virtual server".

In-House

This is the route that gives you most control over your Internet presence, but it will also entail the greater amount of expenditure.

You will need your own server, communications port, and associated software. While you may already have the first two items and there is adequate freely-available server software to be found on the Internet, you will find that costs can easily spiral upwards once you start looking for quality. Only a large business should consider this move, as often it is not necessary and will also require you to hire some technical staff. If you do take this step, you should try to source multitask staff (i.e. someone who can not only maintain your server, but also build your web site).

ISP (Internet Service Provider)

The second alternative, and the most attractive to most new business on the Internet will be the rental of space on someone else's server - the same one you use to connect to the Internet. Most ISPs now offer free web space to their clients, but you should check the following criteria:

1. Do they allow commercial sites? Many don't.
2. How many changes are you allowed to make to your web pages per month?
3. How much disk space is available for your files? This varies from two to 20Mb and sometimes up - but often 5Mb is more than enough.
4. How easy is it for you to upload/change the files that are used to create your web pages?
5. What security is in place to prevent others tampering with your pages?
6. Is there a limit to the number of visitors or hits you can receive on your pages?

7. What technical support can the ISP offer? You'll need it if you're building your own web site.
8. Are any design services available? Be careful here, this is often the 'cream' for the ISP, and you may get charged through the nose.
9. What is your ISP's connection record like? It is no good having a cheap deal if your customers can never get onto your web site because the ISP server is constantly overloaded or breaking down.
10. How long has the ISP been in business? Remember the Internet is a growth area and further ISPs are springing up all over the place with varying degrees of experience - so beware of cowboys.
11. Can I buy a domain name through the ISP or use a domain name I have bought elsewhere for my web space? Technically this is very easy to do, but many smaller - and even some large 'bulk' ISPs - try to discourage this as they sell domain names and get snotty about you finding a better deal elsewhere. Again, they often count on this for more cream.

Virtual Servers

Virtual server companies either rent or sell space for the storage of web pages. The advantage of having a virtual server for your web pages is that it allows you to change your ISP (which you will still need to connect to the Internet, collect your email etc.) without your web address having to change.

Mind you, this is also the case if you have a domain name, which is why many Virtual Servers offer deals that include hosting and a domain name of your choice. You should be careful here about signing long term contracts, and also ask many of the same questions you would of an ISP.

Happily, you have plenty of time to search for the right virtual server deal if you choose to do so, as it has no impact on your original connection to an ISP.

Some quick-thinking folks in the United Kingdom have bought thousands of .co.uk domain names to make a great virtual email service called 'Funmail'. It works just like the famous, free US email service Hotmail, but because Funmail make these thousands of domain names available free to their users it lets you be *plumber@steadyleak.co.uk* or *help@writersblock.co.uk* instead of plain old john156@hotmail.com. Once you choose an email address it is yours 'forever', (so long as you use it every 90 days) thus making it a great way for small businesses to secure a snappy email address for stationery and other promotional uses without the expense of securing a domain name.

Once you get your first point of contact, you can, of course, answer them with your direct email address and carry on as normal. A virtual email service of any kind is worth investigating, especially if you wish to make an enquiry or comment on the Internet but do not wish to have the reply address connected to your business.

www.funmail.net

Chapter 9

Building Your Own Web Site

If you can type and save a document on your computer, then you can build a web page. Even better, if you own a PC, there are hundreds of programs available that are absolutely free and in the right hands can produce a page that is indistinguishable from one made 'professionally'.

You should keep in mind, however, that even the finest tools need the right hands. In the end, it's up to you (or a member of your staff) to make the most of it. You can pretty much guarantee that if the person building the web site is capable of making a brochure or pamphlet, then they will be more than capable of building a great web site. They just have to be aware of the five most important rules of web design.

If you would like to know more about this subject, you may like to purchase a copy of *Create Your Own Website* also published by Net.Works. More details can be found at **www.net-works.co.uk**

Rule 1 - Less is More (More or Less)

Every web page you build is fighting the clock. If you put too many graphics or other bells and whistles on your site, then it will take too long to load and you may lose your target's attention before the page has loaded. Remember - one click and they are gone.

Also, while having enough content to capture interest, you should not make the common mistake of writing too much material. It is tempting to think of a web site as 'endless' space, because you are no longer restricted by page size, printing costs etc. - but you must keep in mind that the average web user has a very short attention span. If you do have a lot of content that is necessary to the effective promotion of your business, (like a product or price listing) then it is important to break it up and organise it so it can be viewed in short and easily accessible 'chunks'.

Rule 2 - Well Organised = Easy to Use

Wherever the user is in the site, they should be able to get back to the main page - or any other main section of the site - with one click. No part of the site should be any more than five clicks away from another. It sounds restrictive, but if you want your pages to form a truly functional site you want users to:

- Arrive
- Find what they're looking for
- Use your business

Of course, when your site is acting as an online brochure, (like when you send a link of your site to a potential client) then you want them to have a good poke around. But again, if they don't get the message within a few clicks they will quickly tire of the exercise.

Rule 3 - Strong Code = Good Site

Strictly speaking, you don't need to learn HTML, (the code behind web pages) but a strong authoring program and some knowledge of the workings of HTML will be required to make your site as functional as possible. If you have a very basic web authoring program, (i.e. a free one) and absolutely no knowledge of HTML you should not try to get too fancy, or the whole deck of cards will fall down and certain people will not be able to see your site at all. Once you've built a page or two, have a look at the code the authoring program has generated for you (you may be surprised at how easy it is to understand). When you see an effect or 'look' you like on somebody else's web page, try right-clicking on it and selecting 'View Source' to see their HTML code - you would be surprised how many tricks you can pick up on in this way.

Rule 4 - Words Don't Come Easy

Writing good copy is hard at the best of times, but on the web you are dealing with a more sophisticated, and often more jaded, audience. You should not simply lift the copy from your latest brochure and put it straight to your web site (though you would be surprised how many blue chip companies still make this mistake).

The copy on your web site should be warm and personable, as you are nearly always playing to an audience of one. You do not need to compromise your corporate integrity to do this, in fact, you should be very careful not to go too far with it and commit the ultimate sin: "Hi, my name is David and welcome to my web site" (shudder). Also, you should never 'oversell' your product or make unrealistic claims, lest you be grouped with those pariahs of the web - Spammers.

Being a Copywriter by trade it would be remiss of me not to say 'hire a professional' - after all, I need the money - but if you have researched the web well enough there is no reason why you shouldn't be able to draft the written content of your pages yourself. A warning here, if you hire a professional design company to make your site, do not automatically assume that they have a professional writer on staff. Getting a programmer or designer to write copy for your site is not unlike getting the printer to do it for your brochure.

Rule 5 - First Impressions Last

Even if your site-building abilities have nothing to do with the kind of goods or service on offer, users would like to think that you are a company they can respect. This means producing a page that gives an impression of quality. It's a little like turning up to a meeting unshaven and wearing torn jeans, (you may be the very best at what you do, but if a suit is called for you wear a damn suit - purely because it makes the right impression). The last thing you want to do is give users the idea that you care so little about your business, as they will assume that you care even less about your customers. Take pride in your work, and do the job right.

Basic Web Site Structure

The Home Page

Your 'home page' - or index page - is like the front page of a newspaper or a cover of a magazine. At a glance it should portray what your business is about and what further information may be found on other pages of the site.

The Net.Works
home page at:
www.net-works.co.uk
has to look good and
grab the visitor's
attention quickly

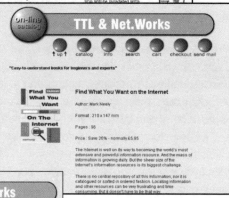

Product information on
the second level can be
more expansive.

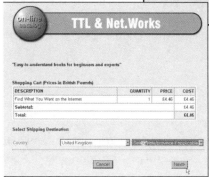

A secure shopping area will remove
many visitor's fears.

While anyone can enter your web site at any point, most people will enter via the home page. And since first impressions count double, you will find that your company will often be judged solely on this page - particularly so by people who are not familiar with your company's name (which will be most web users, given the global nature of the Internet).

On this page you should not only include your company name and logo, but also direct contact details such as telephone and fax numbers, email addresses, and a "snail mail" address. It is amazing how many companies still produce home pages that do not give the casual browser any way of contacting them outside of the Net, or bury their contact details in an obscure section of the site. If, in your opinion, these details make your home page too busy and detract from your initial impact or primary message, then at least make it very plain as to where in the site they can find these details. A nice big button titled 'Contact' among your navigation choices is widely seen as the standard.

Also include your very best information, but omit the detail. These will act like teasers and encourage readers to delve deeper. One simple testimonial or mission statement and a few extracts should be more than enough. After all, you don't want your customers hanging around the shop front when all of the action is inside the store.

The main purpose of your home page should be to get people to your site, and to encourage them to see more. It is this page you will be submitting to search engines, apart, of course, from your generative pages (see below).

Those who are interested will be grateful for a clear signpost, and those who aren't will be thankful for you not wasting their time. Any recent changes you have made can be flagged by a symbol or flash showing that an item has been updated or added to the site. This will draw the attention of regular visitors and let them know that something new has arrived worth looking at. Otherwise they may assume it is the same as the last time they visited and immediately depart. Your home page should, most importantly, have navigation choices, (ideally on the left or top of the page) that well let them get to all of the other major sections of your site with one click.

Other Pages

There are many practical benefits to repeating the same basic graphics on the pages of your web site, (these are discussed below) but the other main reason for this is to give a feeling of decor and style. If you wish to clearly identify different sections, you can do so simply by prominent titles and/or colour.

It is best to follow the example of newspapers and magazines when it comes to the body text of your work pages. Put your best information at the top and get home all your important points. Most people will only get a third to half way down your page before hitting a link or returning to where they came from, and they may miss any nuggets that appear at the end of a poorly constructed page. As you go down the page you can afford to be more general in your writing and start including more detail as necessary. It is probably safe to assume that only the most interested will reach the bottom of a particular story.

Start out by studying other web sites to see how it is done. Then sit down and decide on the approach you wish to take, the purpose of going on-line, and the goals you want to achieve. After this, you can make a positive decision to start small and aim to expand (making sure that you understand how your site could expand), remember Rome was not built in a day. By 'small', consider no more than two or three pages, with one solitary page being a good option.

Build a story that you want your visitors to follow, and construct a route plan around your web site. Then organise how you wish to give the information in the same manner that you would in a formal presentation, bearing in mind your target market.

Generative Pages

If your concept involves pages of useful information for other surfers or other positive qualities that web users are likely to be seeking (and therefore *generating* traffic), it should be similarly outfitted with all of the major features of the home page – giving the user a feeling of continuity.

Links Pages

A links page is a page of links to other sites on the web that you consider beneficial to your customers.

> **Tip**
>
> **Golden Clicks**
>
> A Golden rule of thumb, which should be followed when constructing your web site, is to not make any location more than five mouse clicks away from any other location.

These links are going to be of high importance to your readers, so make sure you put a lot of effort into understanding where your typical customer may wish to jump off to.

Some web site owners find visitors coming to their site purely for the quality of their links (in fact, an effective links page can be a great generative site in itself, but the links will have to be carefully selected and include a fitting description of the site involved). The visitors may have very little intention of lingering around the site in question and might often merely using it as a blast off point for other locations around the web. This is not always a bad thing, as the more traffic you have on a site the higher you will be placed in many search engines.

Shopping Pages

If you wish to trade directly from your site, (i.e. enable customers to buy your products over the Internet) then the pages involved with the actual transaction will have to be as simple and as functional as possible. The practice of selling directly over the Internet is known as 'E-commerce', and the major issues are covered in Chapter 12.

The Tools You Will Need

The tools listed overleaf may change, as the web moves pretty fast. If you are in any doubt as to your best software options, just visit www.net-works.co.uk/run.htm for the latest and greatest options available to you.

Any material you do save that you wish to be an active part of your final site should be saved into one folder (any conceptual ideas, test pages, artwork, masters etc. should be saved elsewhere). The reasons for this will be obvious later.

Web Authoring Software

The latest version of Internet Explorer comes with free web authoring software known as 'FrontPage Express'. Mac users needn't panic, as the rival browser Netscape also has authoring software known as 'Composer'.

You should keep in mind however, that while very useful, they can be somewhat limiting. There are many other web authoring packages that are available for free from the web, and Microsoft Word also incorporates web-authoring functionality. If you already have and use a recent version of Word, you will find the transition to building web pages an absolute breeze. (If you plan on sending and receiving a lot of documents on the web, you should have this anyway. It is widely regarded as the main word processing software for documents transferred over the Net - for Mac or PC).

Basically, you type, you format, and you save the page as a HTML document in your special web page folder. If you have more than one page to show, you link them together into a series of pages known as a web site. The most important thing to remember here is that the name of the main page - the page you want users to see first - is named 'index' or 'home' (check which with your webspace provider).

Graphics Software

If you so choose, you can source all of your graphics from other web sites, but you should be aware that:

- Many sites, even ones offering 'free graphics' will object to you using them for commercial purposes
- You want to have as many original graphics on your page as possible to give a good impression

With this in mind, a good graphics program is essential for a truly original and elegant look. Paint, the graphics program that comes free with Windows is acceptable, but very restrictive. There are many more free programs available for download that allow you to do more, but as the look of

> **Tip**
>
> If you have had stationery, brochures etc. printed in the past, ask your printer for copies of your logo and any related graphics on disk.

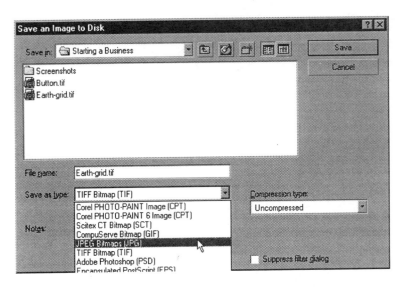

*When saving your graphics for publication
to the web always save as either a JPEG or GIF and,
if possible, compress them as small as you can -
below 10k is the best option*

your site is all-important it may be worth investing in a professional package. A scanner or digital camera may also be a wise investment, especially if you wish to put pictures of your products on your web site. Any graphics that you do wish to be on your web site should be:

- Small (i.e. below 10K)
- Saved as a JPEG or GIF file

The reason for the small file size should be obvious – you don't want your visitors to get bored waiting for it to download and decide to click away to another site. Always design for the lowest common denominator and assume your visitors have a slower modem than you do. JPEGS are best for black and white images or photos, GIFs are best for bright primary colours or the basic frames of an animation. Try timing how long it takes each graphic to appear (at a busy time for the Internet) once you have your site up and running.

> **Tip**
>
> Repeating the same graphics, (like logos, navigation buttons and backgrounds) on all of your pages is a smart move, as most web users have their browser set to store graphics they have already downloaded in a temporary file known as a 'cache'. Essentially, what you are doing is creating many different pages that point to the same graphics, so once web users have successfully downloaded one page containing them, subsequent pages will load much faster.

Animation Software

Again, less is more. You should probably restrict your animation to one a page - preferably your logo or an aspect of it. Try not to make it too long, (too many frames) as your primary branding will take too long to load and many people won't see it.

Animations are very easy to make with the right software - and this is often free, even if it is only for a trial period. You can find links to the best options available to you on this publications web page.

FTP 'Client'

An FTP 'client' is the tool that lets you publish your finished pages to your web space. There are many free versions of this available for download, the most widely used being WS_FTP.

The reason you have saved all of your web page elements into one folder is because when you load it up to your web space it will be in - you guessed it - it's own special folder. Note: as you become more experienced you can experiment with relative addressing, which allows you to put different elements in their own folders on the server, but that is way too advanced for this publication.

If your site has 'links' to other pages or some more complex code, it may not seem to function properly when viewed 'offline' - you will need to upload it to the server to test it properly. Don't worry, no one knows where it is yet, so unless you have a URL that someone is likely to try out (like a formal domain name, for instance) then nobody will be able to see it but you.

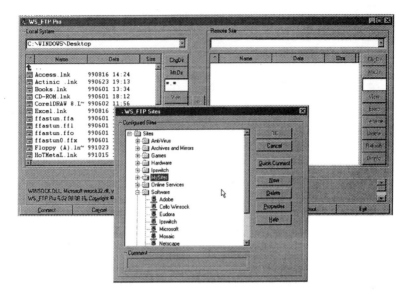

*WS_FTP is one of the most widely used
File Transfer Programmes*

Once your page is built, beautiful and fully tested, it is time to let the world know where it is - but first, we need to dig into the code and put in the most important elements - the META tags.

Tip

It is always a good idea to give ask a few friends to look at your pages once you've loaded them up, but not gone 'live', for their opinions. Often they may say a graphic is missing or a line appears odd in their browser. The missing graphic may appear in *your* browser because it is resident in your cache. This effect can 'con' you into thinking everything is in place, when it really isn't.

Chapter 10

Getting Found

META Tags

META Tags are essential sections in the 'head' of a HTML document that let the search engines know what your page is about. It's kind of like a digital library card that guides people searching for the kind of information you are offering, to your page, and is composed of three major parts:

- **Title** - the formal name of the page
- **Description** - A short description of what the page is about
- **Keywords** - relevant words pertaining to the subject matter of your site

If you want people to be able to find your page, you will have to insert this information into your HTML code. First you will have to put some thought into what your tags will say, so it's probably best to create these in a straight word processing document first, so you can chop and change them without fear of messing with your code.

Once you have done all of this, you will have to insert them into your HTML code, but rest assured, this process is quite easy. All you have to do is open your page in your web authoring software and choose 'View Source' or 'View HTML' from the options provided, paste in your META Tags, then save the page after the changes are made.

The 'Title' isn't formally a META Tag, but it is just as important and a perfect place to start, as we can show you how easy altering HTML can be.

Changing the Title

Remember the page that we told you to name 'index' or 'home'? Well, that has more to do with the right *file* name - the *title* of the page can be anything you like. You probably will have seen a few pages titled 'index' on

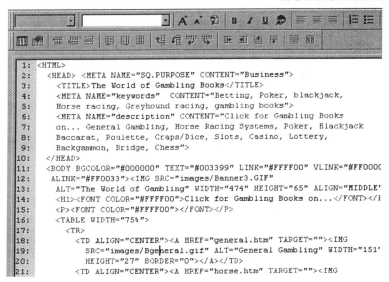

```
 1: <HTML>
 2:   <HEAD> <META NAME="SQ.PURPOSE" CONTENT="Business">
 3:     <TITLE>The World of Gambling Books</TITLE>
 4:     <META NAME="keywords" CONTENT="Betting, Poker, blackjack,
 5:     Horse racing, Greyhound racing, gambling books">
 6:     <META NAME="description" CONTENT="Click for Gambling Books
 7:     on... General Gambling, Horse Racing Systems, Poker, Blackjack
 8:     Baccarat, Roulette, Craps/Dice, Slots, Casino, Lottery,
 9:     Backgammon, Bridge, Chess">
10:   </HEAD>
11:   <BODY BGCOLOR="#000000" TEXT="#003399" LINK="#FFFF00" VLINK="#FF000C
12:   ALINK="#FF0033"><IMG SRC="images/Banner3.GIF"
13:     ALT="The World of Gambling" WIDTH="474" HEIGHT="65" ALIGN="MIDDLE'
14:   <H1><FONT COLOR="#FFFF00">Click for Gambling Books on...</FONT></I
15:   <P><FONT COLOR="#FFFF00"></FONT></P>
16:   <TABLE WIDTH="75%">
17:     <TR>
18:       <TD ALIGN="CENTER"><A HREF="general.htm" TARGET=""><IMG
19:         SRC="images/Bgeheral.gif" ALT="General Gambling" WIDTH="151'
20:       HEIGHT="27" BORDER="0"></A></TD>
21:       <TD ALIGN="CENTER"><A HREF="horse.htm" TARGET=""><IMG
```

An example of the Title and META tags used by **The World of Gambling** *on their books page at* **www.gamble.co.uk.** *Turn to page 71 to see how these appear on the Lycos Search Engine.*

your travels through the web; this often results from people either neglecting to change the page title, or being unable to. You can imagine the bad impression this makes on seasoned web users, but we're going to show you how to fix it.

Open the HTML code and look in the 'head' of the document that appears (this is at the very top of the document and easy to find). You will most likely see text like this:

<TITLE>index</TITLE>

You'll see the 'index' text in between the code. Simply replace this text with a better title as shown, (being very careful not to change the code around it) then save your web page.

<TITLE>Taking Care of Business</TITLE>

Now when you open your web page in a browser, you will see that it has a much more descriptive title.

You have just successfully altered your HTML. Next, we're going to show you how to use these skills to add the most important element of your page - 'META Tags'.

As we said, it is probably best to develop these in a plain document first, so if anything goes wrong you don't run the risk of ruining your code.

Note - when you save the word processing document, make sure you put it somewhere handy, but DO NOT save it to your special web page folder.

Adding META Tags

The two Meta-Tags you will need for your page are:

1)   A selection of KEYWORDS - this allows the search engine to decide how relevant your site is when a 'keyword' query is made.

2)   A short DESCRIPTION of the contents within the site - this appears as part of the search results offered for each query and helps the searcher to choose the best page from the results listed.

Keywords

The code required is: <META NAME="KEYWORDS" CONTENT="keywords, here, separated, by, commas, and, a, space, relevant groups of words, can be grouped, without commas, if desired">

Example: A plumber may have <META NAME="KEYWORDS" CONTENT="plumbing, plumber, water, pipes, piping, emergency, leak, seep, pour, trickle">

Tip

You would be surprised how many 'typos' are made when searching. Try including a few misspellings of vital words amongst your keywords. Have a look at the keywords your competition are using and try to think of a few they have missed. If you have any pages that involve different material from that of your main site, then you should come up with as many new words as possible for these pages.

68

Put some thought into your keywords and include as many different synonyms and related words concerning your product, company or subject as you can think of. You are allowed around 30 keywords per page.

Description

The code required is: <META NAME=" DESCRIPTION " CONTENT="type your description here">

You are allowed about 1,000 characters for your description, but not all these will be displayed, so try to include the most important descriptive information *first.*

Once your tags are complete, highlight and 'Copy' the text, then open your web pages and 'Paste' ('Ctrl' and 'V') the code into the 'head' of the HTML just under the 'Title'. You will see your META-Tags have been inserted into the 'head' of the HTML 'code'. Save your web page to disk, then re-open your web page in your browser. Click the 'Refresh' button on the toolbar, then select 'Source' from the pull-down 'View' menu. You should see your tags in place, even if they have been moved and changed slightly by the authoring program. Don't worry, this is normal and different authoring programs put them in different places (some even have their own META Tags, that they insert to show which program the page was made with). Once your META Tags are in place and you are ready to submit your web page to search engines.

Submitting to Search Engines.

If you've been on the web for a while and maybe submitted an article or two to a newsgroup, then you will no doubt have received a Spam along the lines of 'WE WILL SUBMIT YOUR SITE TO OVER 1000 SEARCH ENGINES FOR ONLY $89.95'. This is a blatant rip-off, as it is something you can quite easily do for yourself. Also, most businesses will only need to submit their main web pages to about a dozen or so major search engines and maybe a few smaller ones that relate specifically to their locale, trade or subject matter.

The only pages on your site that you need to submit to the search engines are your home page and any generative or links pages that you consider to be of value or relevant to a certain search engine. (For instance, if you had a page relating to the history of Scotland, then you would submit this page separately to any Scottish search engines with its own special description and keywords.)

Main Search Engines

To start with, it's probably best just to register with one or two engines manually. To do this, go to each search engine in turn and look for a link on their main page saying 'Add URL' or 'Submit URL'. Follow this link to the submission form and submit your page. Different engines require different levels of information, but for the most part all they will ask for is the URL (individual web address) of the page and your email address (so they can confirm the entry of your page into their database or alert you of any problems).

If you are not sure what your URL is, check with the information from your ISP. The easiest way to make sure the URL is correct is to view your web page online and 'Copy' the entire text that appears in the 'Address' window of your browser. You can then 'Paste' this text into the submission form at the search engine(s) of your choice.

There are also a few pages around that let you submit to multiple search engines at once. There will be links to the best of these at www.net-works.co.uk/run.htm.

It will take a few days (and sometimes a few weeks) for your engine to be included in the search engine database, so be patient. The easiest way to check if you are included in a search engine's database is to type your entire URL in the 'Search' box and click 'Search'. If you're in there, it will find you.

Once your entry appears, you will see how useful your 'Description' META-Tag is to people looking for your page. It is these few words that often mean the difference between people choosing your site over another search engine result.

The reason we have advised you to only submit to one or two engines at first is because you may feel you need to make a few changes to your 'Description' after you have viewed it in action. You will almost definitely wish to change a thing or two about your site in this time, so this 'cooling off' period is more of a blessing than a curse. If you make any changes to your META Tags, you will have to re-submit the related

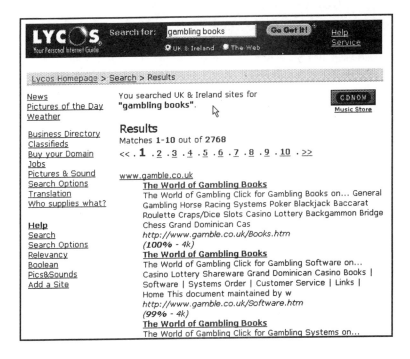

An excellent result for **The World of Gambling** at Lycos. A search for 'Gambling Books' produced the top six hits. See how these results have been produced by the title and META tags shown on page 67.

---

page to the search engines so the latest version of the 'Description' will appear in the search results.

(Note - you won't have to re-submit your page each time you change it, only when you alter the META Tags.)

You may also want to play around with your keywords a bit after a few experiments. To find out how useful (or suitable) your keywords are, try typing a few of the words you have used and see what kind of 'ranking' you get for different combinations of these words.

Once you have settled on a good description and some powerful keywords, then you can submit your new page far and wide with confidence.

Specialised Search Engines

Sometimes web users will go to a search engine that only lists sites of a certain kind, or from a certain locality.

The best way to find which of these search engines exist is to go to a site like www.finderseeker.com, which lets you search for search engines. Once you find anything that relates to your particular business or locality, submit your page.

Local Directories

Remember the local directories you found when you did your initial research? You should also submit your site to them - and any other local or trade directory you can find that is free. Even though it often takes much less time to get your pages listed in such directories, you should probably try to time it so these listings go live around the same time as those of the search engines. As we said, some form of 'cooling off' period is necessary, as you will find many things you wish to change once your site is live.

Now key pages from your site are listed with the major search engines, the world will beat a path to your door, right? Well, not always. Sites equally relevant to yours, but with higher traffic, tend to be placed higher in the search results. Usually, if you do not end up in the top 10 or 20 results you will be missed by the majority of users, and here lies the biggest Catch-22 of the web. High results in search engines will get you a lot of traffic, but often you need traffic to get those high results.

With a good generative concept, you are well on the way to achieving this. As traffic is often calculated by site and not by page, even a completely unrelated page that results in a lot of hits to your site will result in your other pages placing higher in completely unrelated searches.

However, to get the ball rolling you will need to do a little active marketing.

Chapter 11

Actively Marketing Your Web Site

There are many ways to immediately increase your web site traffic, but some should most definitely be treated with caution.

With a Grain of Salt

Swapping Links

If you include a link on your page to somebody else's page they may agree to provide a link in the opposite direction, particularly if there is some synergy between the sites. Occasionally you will come across the owner of a site who believes his traffic level is larger than yours, so he may feel that you should pay a fee in addition to swapping links. This is not recommended and you should simply walk away from the deal.

Lottery Resources

- The World of Gambling - Free gambling hints, tips and systems from horse racing to blackjack.
- 2b - Lottery Results by Email
- DT Lotto Database - Aussie lottery database, also /au.html
- EcoLotto - Shareware lotto program that has wheeling systems for lotto 6/49 games
- Gambling.com - Large selection of lottery and gambling links.
- Gaminco.com - Your online gaming adventure starts here!
- Lotto Edge Magazine - Online info from the US magazine.
- Lotto Factory - Lottery software programs from Aureole Electronic Research
- Lotteries America - Lottery betting from Australia, France, Germany, Ireland, Spain and England.
- Lottery Monitor - Monthly magazine reporting on UK Lottery awards to good causes.
- JT's Systems Shop - JT's Systems newsletter
- Picker - Lottery shareware and registration is $5
- Winninglotto.com - Lottery course by late mathematician Dr. Michael McKinney.

Home . Suggest New Link . Report Dead Link

The Lottery Company swaps links to share traffic with other non-competing lottery related sites - **www.lottery.co.uk**

Banners

Very large sites make a considerable amount of money selling 'banner' advertising. This can, (and does) get as expensive as television advertising. There has also been a lot of criticism about the effectiveness of banner advertising, so paying to be on a 'big' site may not necessarily pay big dividends. However, if there is a popular site run by a community group, (or even a bunch of keen schoolkids) you may consider sponsoring it in exchange for some exposure. There are also 'banner exchange' programmes that, in exchange for you putting banners on your site, put your banner on other sites. You should keep in mind, however, that these usually work at a 2:1 or 3:1 ratio and you have little control over the nature of the advertising - so again, it pays to be careful.

Web Rings

Joining a 'web ring' of sites on a certain theme is also beneficial, but only to a point. When you join a web ring, you put a link to the ring of sites on your page. Other sites on the ring have similar links, so someone interested in that theme can go through the ring site by site or even choose to see a ring site at random. Generally, this practice is of most benefit to the person who runs the web ring.

Awards

It is much better to give than to receive. Having a bunch of 'awards' on your site will not impress anybody, but having your own awards scheme can pay off - especially if you submit your award to a central awards page. This usually means getting about a dozen emails a week from amateur page builders wanting you to consider their site for your award. Of course, all awards come complete with a link back to your page, so some traffic can build from here. Mind you, often it is just more people after awards.

Competitions

Though most web users are after something 'free', a fair amount of promotion is required for your competition to be effective - putting you back at square one. Also, due to the nature of the web, there are many users, (and whole sites) dedicated to Internet based competitions.

BOOKSHOP CENTRAL
The easy way to find the books you want on the Internet

Play Fantasy Lotto™

Playing **Fantasy Lotto**™ couldn't be easier.

All you have to do is correctly predict both the bonus ball in the main lottery draw on a Saturday and the thunderball on the same day. That's a 1:49 chance, and a 1:14 chance, so your odds of winning are better than those of matching four balls in the main draw.

The prize is a mixed bag of lottery goodies from lottery keyrings, ticket holders, software, pens, lottery card games, lottery dice and a whole selection of lottery books and internet guides. The value of the Fantasy Lottery goody bag will equal that of the prize given away to all match-four tickets on the week in question. So if match-four tickets all win £60, you will receive £60 of Fantasy lotto goodies. If match-four tickets all win £100, you will receive £100 of Fantasy lotto goodies and if match-four tickets all win £250, you will receive £250 of Fantasy lotto goodies, etc.

But the best bit is that playing Fantasy Lotto™ is completely FREE. So you can win the same value as a match-four lottery ticket. The odds of winning are better AND you don't have to pay to enter!

A free-to-enter online competition can increase traffic dramatically - another example from **www.lottery.co.uk**

The end result is usually a bunch of folks slavering after the freebies and with little interest in your business. You may also consider the 'capture data' from competitions to be of some value, but for the most part the only information you can count on to be correct is the email address.

Do So at Your Peril

email 'Spamming'

If the purpose of your 'Emailout' is to get people who have never heard of you before to come and visit your site then - like it or not - you will be guilty of Spamming. This is one of the most unpopular methods of promotion on the web, and thus one of the least effective. Also, you usually have to pay for lists of email addresses and get special software to run the mass mailout - and in the end you will probably get more mail telling you where to go than you will from people asking you where you are. Spamming just isn't worth the heartache. Don't do it.

However, do not be put off using email to contact businesses or people you already know of, or even local businesses you have found on your online travels. A short, friendly email along the lines of, "Hello, we are now on the web" will do you no harm at all - but check your spelling.

Newsgroup 'Spamming'

The other easy route to Internet advertising is via Newsgroups. However, as we have noted earlier you have to be extremely careful. Putting your details in a newsgroup is rather like walking on thin ice as almost all promotions of goods and services are considered an advertisement by newsgroup users. You may not see it that way, but then you are no longer in charge of what is considered an advertisement or not. In the real world the definitions are very clear. If you pay for space it's an advertisement, if it's free you are gaining publicity. But on the Internet the perception is in the eyes of a reader, and if they think it is an ad, then it IS an ad.

All of this talk of offending people in Newsgroups is not just scare mongering. Flames are not just simply abusive messages received on the Internet. They are warnings that your tactics are offending other users. And if not dealt with correctly they can easily escalate into a situation that could harm your Internet activities forever. For example, if a flame-thrower is sufficiently annoyed to ask two of his friends to flame your business, who ask two of their friends, who ask two of their friends, you can see how a cascade of email can cripple your server. And if you think how easy it is for you to automate your outgoing emails, it is equally as easy for the flame-throwers to automate their mailings to you over a long period.

Spamming (posting off-subject notices in a newsgroup) will not only attract the attentions of the Cancelbot but it could get you barred from a group or set of groups. Some of the worst offences of inappropriate advertising can see you placed into a black list or have your account closed by your Internet access provider.

Subject	From	Sent	Size
FA Premier League Football Manager 2000	Vernon Moorhouse	02/11/99 01:56	4KB
FANTASY LEAGUE	Aaron Best	04/11/99 10:14	1KB
FIFA 2000 Info?	Martin Sharp	26/10/99 06:49	1KB
FIFA 2000 Speech	Zeke Wolfy	28/10/99 01:10	2KB
Football statistics	mapfumo	29/10/99 07:01	1KB
GALATASARAY 3 AC Milan 2	Ludwig	04/11/99 07:35	1KB
How to shoot a deadball in FIFA2000? Pleas...	Superunknown	08/11/99 02:32	1KB
Italy or England???	ross cathie	01/11/99 10:50	1KB
JUVENTUS F.C. site	Cathy Eng	01/11/99 02:37	2KB
Leeds United FC - Welcome to Elland Road	Iain S Cummings	26/10/99 11:33	2KB
Looking for sport games you can spectate	Martin Sharp	26/10/99 06:42	1KB
Lowest Prices On New & Used Games 5302	mwmjhr@excite.com	26/10/99 08:03	1KB
Michael Owen World League Soccer 2000?	Anders Jørgensen	30/10/99 05:04	1KB
Promotion is doubtful at Hillsbro'	Peter Naldrett	31/10/99 11:50	1KB
Rosenborg	Turjan	26/10/99 08:12	1KB
Soccer????	logsnet	02/11/99 04:34	1KB
The best page the Soccer in America Latina ...	aficionada	31/10/99 12:40	2KB
THE BEST TEAM SOCCER LATINO?	analista	04/11/99 06:50	1KB
Tips for PSX Games?	ML	01/11/99 08:16	1KB
watches	foot	25/10/99 07:17	1KB
Re: What do you think about FIFA 2000?	Zeke Wolfy	04/11/99 03:42	2KB

Obvious Spam   Possible Spam

Examples of spam in a newsgroup which is supposed tio be about soccer. Note how spammers rarely use their names.

After all these warnings you may be surprised to find that there are Newsgroups that do allow advertising. In a community as large as the Internet, you are bound to get specific advertisement Newsgroups. Most of these begin with the prefix biz.marketplace followed by the subject of the newsgroup e.g. biz.marketplace.communications.telephones and biz.marketplace.international. You should feel free to blatantly advertise in these Newsgroups, but do remember to keep on-topic and be aware that your post will be buried under thousands of other advertisements.

There are also Newsgroups dedicated specifically to 'classifieds'. Just what makes a classified on the Internet is not very clear, since all email and newsgroup postings have the textural appearance of a classified (of course the web is an exception). Each of these groups will include the identifier: classified, for sale, or market place.

They fall into two categories, those defined by locality and those specific to a product. For example, you may come across uk.marketplace and fj.marketplace for classified advertisements only relevant to the UK and Japan, or you may find some product specific groups such as rec.computers.marketplace.

A Final Warning - Even if you think you know what a particular newsgroup is for, always check the FAQs and spend some time reading messages within the group before posting your own. As a mark of politeness it is also recommended that you include the word "AD" in the subject line of your message. Then to make doubly sure that users can't mistake your posting for a Spam by explaining in the first paragraph exactly how it relates to the topic of the newsgroup. The rest of the text should be subtle (time and again test advertising on the Internet has shown that the hard sell does not work). As part of the subtler approach you should also try to limit the number of exclamation marks you use!!!, the quantity of ****asterixes**** which will make your message look awful and never use CAPITALS which is the email and newsgroup equivalent of SHOUTING IN SOMEONE'S EAR WITH A MEGAPHONE!!!!!

With the Sweat from Your Brow

Newsgroup 'Lurking'

They say the cheapest and currently most financially rewarding form of marketing on the Internet is that of 'lurking'. This involves regular visits to Newsgroups and fora (plural of forum!) as a visitor, or as a member, and a sharp eye for that potential future customer.

The most successful Net lurkers are usually experts in their field. They familiarise themselves with all the Newsgroups and on-line service fora where they would normally expect to find customers for their line of business. Then they offer free advice to users of the group in the hope of creaming off business at a later stage. A favour today, is an Internet sale tomorrow.

Most lurkers enter Newsgroups as an individual as opposed to a representative of a company. This involves having a non-traceable email address, (see Chapter 8) and not using a signature file at the end of their messages. However, in some sectors, most notably the professions, being identified as an expert can have a positive effect - as does a link to your home page in your signature file.

Whichever way they enter a group, all good Net lurkers have one thing in common. They give regular and useful information free of charge to other users of the group. It is in this manner that their name becomes respectable and the users come to trust the advice that they are being given. This in turn can then lead to sales through carefully placed references to your company's products or services.

If you do decide to use Net lurking as a way of generating sales you must take extra care not to contravene 'netiquette' (see Appendices) or to go against the Newsgroups' own rules. In particular you should only give details of where the users can get hold of your products OR to give the price, but not details of where they can get them AND the price. This may sound like nit picking but it is a clearly defined line between a useful message and blatant advertising. Pass it and you will be abused, or play safe and be respected.

Finally, make sure you do read the rules of each Usenet group which can usually be found in the FAQs. There you can perhaps save a lot of time by finding out if advertising is allowed in the group, (some do allow straightforward advertising that is relevant) or whether no commercial references are allowed at all.

Starting Your Own Newsgroup

You should only go down this rather drastic route if a Usenet group does not already exist close to your existing sector. For example, if you deal in a highly specialised area such as fibreoptics you may see a need for a Usenet group called biz.fibreoptic.splicers to discuss fusion splicers, heat shrink ovens and cleavers. But if you do go down this route, be prepared for several months going through the various committees necessary to start a Usenet group, and do not forget the ongoing maintenance manpower that will be required.

From the start you will need to cultivate an air of respectability. So you should aim to allow an open discussion of your market place or sector. Allow dialogue on the strength and weaknesses of other manufacturers or the pros and cons of a different technique to your own. If you "moderate" the messages that are allowed to appear, you will probably be seen as a heavy handed censor thus defeating the object of the newsgroup and losing users. Conversely, an open and frank debating chamber can be useful to you as well as others. What is more, dedicated fans will spread the word across the Internet and you are guaranteed to locate several new prospects.

Internet Publicity

The dividing line between marketing, advertising, and publicity are often very narrow in the real world. And the same applies to the Internet. Usually, publicity can be more readily defined as free promotion for your goods and services. However, on the Internet, marketing and advertising can be achieved for next to no cost, if not completely free. So the same definitions do not apply.

Internet publicity tends to be defined instead as the narrower off-line criteria of being aimed at the media. In other words, it should be seen as an attempt to get on-line, and of course off-line, publications to carry details of your products and services.

While Internet opinion is divided, it must be said that at this juncture that most gurus believe Internet publicity seeking to be less successful than real world activities. So unless you are particularly keen, or your business lends itself especially to the Internet (For example,computers or Internet services), then you may want to limit the amount of time and effort that you spend in this direction.

You may already have an existing list of publicity contacts that you use to send regular printed press releases. If possible try making direct contact with these sources and discover if they have an email address. You can then create your very own electronic publicity database. Make sure, though, when speaking to your sources that you ask if they wish to receive email press releases or not. Whilst some journalists, writers and reporters love to receive information in electronic form some positively detest it or wish to keep their email baskets free for personal mail.

You should also use an existing list of customers as a base for a new mailing list especially if you are in the business-to-business sector. Small businesses in particular are more likely to receive your press releases as something positive than an individual, and you are less likely to generate a hostile response. It would be all too easy to include occasional customers and individuals in this list but you are increasing your chances of the shot being badly received. A general rule of thumb would be to only send electronic press releases to those people or companies that you would ordinarily have sent a printed version.

In the Real World

If you are new to the Internet you will not have any problem with this at all, but many seasoned surfers totally forget about one of the most obvious marketing arenas - the real world. Make sure that you not only include your email address on your business cards and letterheads, but also ensure that your Internet site details appear somewhere in your printed advertisements and brochures. It is, after all, something to be proud of. By letting people know that you are on the Internet it is a way of showing your customers and new prospects that you are a forward thinking business and up to speed with all existing technology.

Many companies who do remember the real world often simply insert their Internet details as if it were an afterthought in small text at the end of an advertisement or tucked away on the inside back cover of their brochure. Yet, those same companies do not hesitate to shout about their freephone number from the rooftops. Your email address should be given almost as much prominence, and certainly no less respect, than your fax number, when it comes to printed matter and traditional advertisements.

This is the case especially if you have gone to the expense of a domain name. This should be on every piece of paper, vehicle and product that goes out of your office.

Some Promotion Warnings

Flash Crowds

Perhaps your biggest enemy, when it comes to Internet marketing, is the possibility of total success. Because you are broadcasting to such a large audience and since responses can be almost instantaneous, getting it right can be a frightening experience. An Internet phenomenon known as a 'flash crowd' can descend upon your Internet site totally crippling all of its functions.

This is because word of mouth travels at a frightening pace on the Internet. It is so easy for somebody to pass on details of your goods and services via an email message, simply by hitting the forward button when they are reading the original reference. You may also find other individuals or businesses with Web and Internet sites of their own creating hypertext or other links straight to your site. And then, if you have created something new or interesting, you may find yourself placed in one of the Internet's top 10 site lists, what's new on the Internet reviews, or cool site lists (this is just what a successful press release can do).

However, when the crowd descends you need to be in a position to deal with it. Fortunately, technology can take care of the main burden. If your site is resident on your access provider's machine, this could have enough technology to take care of the surge. And if you run your site from your own computer, a high bandwidth modem should suffice. If you have neither of these, your site may not be capable of responding to anyone who wants to make a visit. For sure you will lose some potential customers, but do not be tempted into making rash changes to your system unless you know what you are doing. It may sound easy to whip out your old modem and replace it with one of a higher bandwidth. But the practicalities of such an operation can throw up several problems you had not anticipated. Needless to say a slow loading site is better than a site which does not load at all, so in this situation you must simply shrug your shoulders and accept what is happening (but do not forget to at least pat yourself on the back for the marketing success).

The rest of the effort needed to deal with flash crowds will consist of raw manpower. You should endeavour to respond to all emails and visitors on the same day if possible and certainly within two. If you do not have enough existing resources then you should seek outside assistance from an agency. Surfers expect a quick response and any delay could disappoint more than it would in the real word.

Keeping Up the Content

Once your World Wide Web site is up and running it will be very tempting just to sit back and hope that the money rolls in. But that is the very last thing that you can afford to do. It cannot be stressed enough how often you need to make changes to keep your site interesting and encourage those potential customers to return. If you fail to maintain an interesting site it will be your loss, not theirs, since there are literally hundreds of thousands of alternatives for them to visit. Research has shown that if you can afford to change your site everyday you can expect the regulars to return every few days. If you change it every week they will return every few weeks and if you change it every month they will return every few months. So it is up to you how often you think your customers need to see details of your products before they will make that buying decision., and the benefit they feel they've received from each visit.

A Final Warning

If your interest in marketing ideas can truthfully be described as a "scam", think again. I do not say this for any puritanical reasoning. No, the reason for my warning is simply that it will have been done before at least a thousand times. The Internet world has seen everything from the first Spamming incident, where every single Usenet group on the Internet received the same advertisement, to software that scanned users' hard disks for certain key words and resident programs. Cyberspace may be like the wild west in some respects, but there are many battle-hardened veterans out there and always someone quicker on the draw than you.

Chapter 12

Web Counters and Feedback

Web Counters

The most basic feedback you are interested is the number of people who are visiting your site. By comparing this to the number of enquiries you get you can get a pretty good idea of the site's effectiveness. For example, The Lottery Company discovered that the majority of visitors to their site (www.lottery.co.uk) came on a Sunday and a Thursday. They were obviously coming to check their lottery numbers. So the Lottery Company made the lottery results page much better, updated it earlier and changed their lottery news sections on Sunday and Thursday mornings, so that the majority of visitors always saw fresh news.

Most ISPs will have details of basic scripts you can insert into your HTML that will give you a visible counter. These are known as 'CGI' scripts, and the quality of them differs greatly from server to server. Often, you have little control over what the counter looks like, and it only counts general field traffic, rather than letting you know results for separate pages (so you know which are most popular).

A neat solution here is a free service known as LE Fastcounter. When you sign up for this service, you are given a code to post into your HTML that will give a visible result for that page alone. You can get counters for many different pages on the one account, and also choose from a number of different designs depending on your colour scheme. The results are then sent to you by monthly or weekly email, or you can go to their web site and sign into your account to check the weekly results yourself.

Other services offer more complex counters that can give you more complex information like where the traffic is coming from and how long they stay within your site, but these vary greatly in reliability and new and better services are always being introduced. Also, some of them involve complex code that doesn't always work, or is often fatally altered

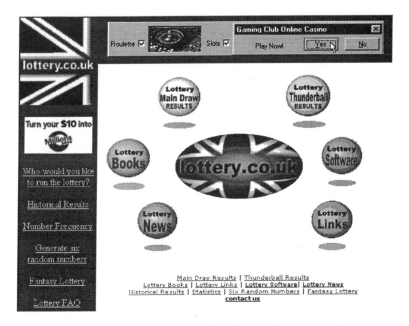

Knowing when visitors come to The Lottery Company's site at **www.lottery.co.uk** *dictate when the site is updated*

by some authoring programs (which do have a tendency to monkey around with other people's HTML). All in all, it's probably best to start out with something simple like Fastcounter, you can find a link to this and other free tracking tools on the *Starting and Running a Business on the Internet* web page.

Feedback

There are also several measures you can take to make sure your finished site is an effective marketing tool rather than just an online brochure.

There is a strong emotional tie between surfers and what they feel as 'their' Internet - more so than between TV viewers and the box in the corner of their living rooms, and between radio listeners and their favourite wavelengths. So you can seek to take advantage of this fact by creating a tie between you and the customers.

One way to do this is to find out how people feel. Try getting some feedback to your marketing cases by creating a dialogue. Perhaps ask people for their comments on what you sent them and build up a profile of the people you are trying to deal with. Secondly, give them control and allow them to make choices. This will help them feel more at ease and help build that emotional tie between you and the Internet community.

These do not have to be fancy choices, just simply an option of where to go within your site and what to see. Amongst the Internet community there is also an overwhelming craving for information. That desire leads people to spend many hours on-line resulting in a certain amount of burn out. So it tends to be companies who create something slightly different who receive all the attention. Unless there is something to catch their interest, the surfers who appeared at the speed of light will also disappear at the same rate.

Web Sites - Natural Feedback

One way to get feedback without the person being aware that they are being 'grouped' is to make your web site somewhat specific for each person. You can achieve this by making it interactive; asking visitors to your site questions as they pass through it and take them to different areas of new information depending on the response that you get to those questions. But don't forget that you must give them the choice of where to go and make them feel in charge. It is a difficult balancing act but one which can be achieved with just a little bit of forethought. There is of course one down side to this form of market research. This stems from the fact that these people are already on your site, so they must have some interest in your company or product in the first place and are not indicative of the Internet population as a whole.

Web Sites - Active Feedback

It is very easy to work a form into your web page, thereby enabling you to capture data in precisely the format that you require for further analysis. A well constructed, and a well thought out web survey will not only gain you the best information, but it can make the web surfer feel at home and comfortable in your site and may tempt them to investigate your company further. Keep in mind, however, that the attention span of the average surfer is notoriously short, so don't go overboard. You often have to offer something in return for their time, so a freebie might help.

Above all, for both of these methods, users like to feel that they are reasonably anonymous, so be careful what you ask. They also like to feel that they have the right to visit your page without a bunch of questions, so don't confront them with a survey immediately - and certainly don't make a condition of entry to the site that they give you 'a few details'.

A good example of feedback is, again, present on the Lottery Company's site at **www.lottery.co.uk**. The company is interested in knowing the physical location of their visitors. Are they mostly from outlying areas or inner cities, affluent areas or blue-collar regions, the UK or overseas? A tempter was obviously needed, so the Lottery Company decided they would offer a list of past lottery results, right back to the start of the National Lottery, in return for filling in a small form. Many users see this information, which can be read into a spreadsheet, as useful for checking old results and analysing the numbers that have come out. So, they are happy to fill in the form.

One final point is that you should beware of the information coming back to you. Unless you are actually posting something out to your visitors, they are prone to giving false names and addresses. The Lottery Company, mentioned above, often receive requests supposedly from names such as *Mr D. Duck, The Pond, Ona Farm, Noneofyourbusiness, Mars*!

Email

Make a catalogue of the number of messages that you receive every day and enter them onto a spreadsheet so that you can analyse them by day, week, month and year.

Also make a note of the country of origin which can be gleamed from the Internet mailing address. Enter next to these the subject headings of the messages.

Very soon and with minimal effort you will be able to build up a profile of who is communicating with your company on the Internet, where they are from, and what their main concerns are.

Surveys

There are two ways of conducting surveys on the Net apart from visitors to your own site. That is through email and Newsgroups.

Email

Sending electronic messages to people and reading their replies is obviously the fastest and cheapest method of conducting market research on the Internet. However it is flawed with difficulties. Make sure you keep your messages short, otherwise they just won't be read. A full survey, even one sent to an established customer, is unlikely to garner a response. A short, friendly question like "by the way, how did you find our site?" at the tail of a reply is more likely to get results.

Newsgroups

These are potentially the most useful sources of market research information to be found on the Net. That is because there are so many Newsgroups that only the experts in each subject tend to inhabit them - so any replies that you do get are more likely to be from highly informed individuals and specialists in their field than from just casual passers by.

However you will need to tread very carefully otherwise you could find the whole thing could blow up in your face before you know what is happening. If your message or request is taken the wrong way you will find yourself inundated with angry replies and misleading answers. So make sure that you not only stick to the rules of 'netiquette', but that you also remember the different religious, cultural, and political backgrounds of the global Internet community.

You should consult the list of frequently asked questions (FAQs). You will find one of these in every newsgroup and they usually define, in straightforward terms, who is allowed to post messages to the group and what content is acceptable. As the title suggests, you will also find the answers to questions that are commonly asked by people within the group.

If you ignore these and blindly ask a question that has been asked a million times before you will either get no answers or the usual flaming.

Perhaps the best way to overcome most of these difficulties is not to use Newsgroups as an organisation at all. Go in as an individual, and for several weeks participate in all the normal functions of the group. Perhaps take part in one or more discussion, and let everyone get used to you being around, before you start asking those questions which will be useful to your market research. Try to keep your questions short and easy to answer.

Internet Market Research Possibilities

Answers you can find on the Internet include:-

1. Who are your prospects.

2. Who are your customers.

3. Which prospects are likely to be turned into customers.

4. Who are your most profitable customers.

5. Who is most likely to come back time and again.

6. What people really think about your company.

7. Why you are losing sales.

8. What your customers think of new products and services.

9. How and where you can advertise effectively.

10. Where you can gain the most (positive) publicity.

11. How big is your potential market. Is it growing or contracting.

12. Who are your competitors, at home and worldwide.

13. How well are they doing.

14. What should you be doing to minimise their threat.

Chapter 13

E-Commerce - How Do I Get Paid?

If you planning on selling goods or services online, your initial reaction may be that it is obvious: your customers simply send you a cheque and you send them the goods. But that would be defeating the whole object of being on the Internet in the first place. First of all the Net is all about instant transactions, whether it be exchanges of emails, downloading of files, or commercial transactions. Also, the Internet is a global network, so imagine the problems of a customer in Zimbabwe sending you a cheque in their local currency to an address in the UK. The banks would be rubbing their hands at the mere thought of the charges they can impose at both ends.

If you are in the business-to-business sector you can afford to go through the process of opening customer accounts. Once established this will allow your regular customers to send orders to your email address, allowing you to process them quicker and give a faster turnaround. If you do go this route, make sure that you establish the address to which orders should be sent, and the names and email addresses of authorised buyers, by traditional methods such as fax or regular mail. Once these are established you should only accept changes, especially to the shipping address, by fax and by mail.

If, however, you are expecting to retail to the public you have very few options other than credit card transactions and digital cash. These you can receive by fax, by phone or directly from the Internet. Again, it is usually best to go for the magic 'one-click' of direct Internet sales. This will involve quite a few resources that are normally beyond that of smaller businesses, but we have a few short cuts for that too. Whichever method you end up choosing you will need to open a special account in order to process the transactions.

Also, and probably most importantly, you should keep pages involving transactions as simple as possible - otherwise you will receive a mess of useless information and lose sales.

Traditional Sales Methods

The simplest way for you to trade via the Internet is by giving your normal phone and fax number, (and your email address) and asking the reader to contact you by one of these methods. This is by far the easiest route for you and gets over many of the security implications of ordering over the Internet. However, it does create a resistance to the casual order.

A second preference here is the downloadable and printable form. This is a form that appears on the screen and can be downloaded to the user's computer. From there, the customer simply sends it to their printer, fills in the details and then faxes it to your premises. These forms should obviously include the necessary details such as name and address, daytime telephone number, products required, the quantity of each item to be sent, and payment details.

Online Sales Methods

The third and most complicated option is to include an on-line form involving a credit card transaction. If you currently have a cardholder-not-present (CNP) merchant account, (i.e. can accept credit cards without a signature) and wish to use it to accept transactions over the Internet, you have one vital step to make - consult a professional.

Trading directly online involves a great deal of professional programming knowledge and should not be undertaken by a novice - especially when there is so much potential loss at stake! Effective online transactions not only involve secure transactions, (for your protection and your customers). This involves a process known as encryption, whereby the details of the transaction are scrambled to ensure they are not intercepted and abused.

Of course, the world is not all black and white.

Shopping Cart software is dropping in price to within possible budgets of small and medium sized enterprises. They are also becoming friendlier to use. Some of the best allow the retailer to set up an online store purely by following a set of 'wizards'. No programming knowledge is

Net.Works use a secure online shopping cart which encrypts customer's credit card details **www.net-works.co.uk**

required, but you do need to know about FTP and relative addressing on the Web.

All you have to do is type the description of your products into a form, tell the program where it can find an image of your product, and then hit the 'upload' button. All the intermediate pages are generated by the program, as are the scripts required to run the software on your host's server. It even performs live tests of the system and server before uploading the majority of your pages to make sure it can email you when an order arrives and that you can access the orders in a secure manner.

Proxy merchant facilities are also available to small businesses, by companies known as 'Online Credit Card Processing Companies'. The cheapest of these involve a 10% cut of each transaction, but when you compare this to the cost of setting up a secure site yourself it is often a smart move for smaller businesses.

These proxies run the whole transaction from their secure servers and send you monthly cheques. All you have to do is set the products and prices for your account, then paste the HTML code they give you into your shopping page(s). Each time you set up a new product or price on your account, you are given a specific HTML code to put next to that product which is, in effect, a 'Buy It' button. Once the customer chooses to buy the product, they go into the secure store to make their transaction. Once a valid transaction is made you immediately get an email letting you know that a sale has been made and where to send the product(s). At the end of the month you get your cheque.

As you do not deal with the customers credit card details in any way, it removes the need for high-end encryption programs. Also, most credit card fraud (not just that on the Internet) is perpetrated by employees who have access to such data. You can help yourself and everyone else by limiting the number of people who are exposed to that information and a proxy system removes this burden from your shoulders.

A word to the wise - do not accept any deals that involve monthly charges unless you are sure of your turnover and know you are onto a better deal. Generally, it is better to live with a percentage-only deal so you do not end up getting charged monthly for a service that makes no sales. Perhaps the best example of a percentage-only deal is that operated by Go-Fun Shopping (www.go-fun.com). This is a loose co-operative of specialist retailers who don't want to get into the technically-difficult area of providing secure online facilities. Go-fun take orders on behalf of the retailers, via their 128-bit encryption system, and then pass them on to the individual retailers in return for a percentage of the total order. The retailer also benefits by not needing any knowledge of the Internet at all!

Be it a proxy service or a professional service you have commissioned directly, your online store should offer the following benefits to you and your customer.

- calculate charges as they go along
- add in carriage or postage charges
- ideally, calculate in the currency of the user
- make the final cost very clear
- automatically generate an acknowledgement to your customer's email account
- transmit the information directly to your fulfilment department
- copy it to your accounting department

Chapter 14

Internet Security - Keeping Out Unwanted Forces

The Internet is an inherently open network. That means merely by joining it your computer becomes exposed to somewhere in the region of 35 million other computers and 150-200 million users. Most of those netizens (citizens of the Internet) are completely law abiding and simply going about their day to day business.

However, as in any community, there is the unwanted criminal element. Your risk of coming across this element is fairly small, nevertheless you should still be on your guard. A pocketful of stories would have you believe that your main danger comes from computer whiz kids, but these are largely blown up beyond all proportion and your worst enemy is undoubtedly the industrial hacker. Such break-ins are likely to go unreported, and indeed most companies who receive hacker's attentions often never find out. They are likely to be working for a direct or indirect competitor of your business, or at least in the same sector. Sometimes they can just be a computer savvy individual who has developed a beef with your company (yet another reason to be careful with Newsgroups and the like).

Every moment you are connected to the Internet, you are technically at risk. During this time, a determined and skilled hacker is able to:

* copy customer files
* corrupt your databases
* browse through your financial accounts
* delete important software
* send false email
* etc, etc.

You could remove 95% of your security worries with two simple measures. First, do not put anything on your Internet server which you would not wish to read on a front page of newspaper - this is not only the information that is easiest to access, but it is 'live' 24 hours a day, leaving much more time for trial and error. Secondly, have a dedicated or stand alone computer for your entire Net activities, keeping all other critical software and information for the day to day running of your business on a separate system.

By doing so you accept that there may be a breach of security but at least only the one computer will be damaged in the process. If you have no alternative but to keep your existing in-house network connected to your Internet server you will need to install a "firewall". This is a sophisticated, and often expensive, suite of software best installed by the experts. It will include routines beyond your wildest technical dreams, all designed to prevent any unauthorised user or software program accessing your system.

However you go about arranging your Internet security - it helps to be paranoid!

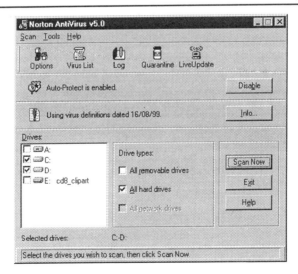

*A good anti-virus package, which can be updated frequently,
is vital for any size of online business*

The Risks

Password Cracking

This is still the most common danger to any computer linked to a network. Attackers essentially guess the password needed to access your system, for which there are even hacking dictionaries available. The problem lies in the fact that humans, who are taught to think logically and emotionally, generate their own passwords and in doing so use very little imagination. Did you know, for example, the two most common passwords are "password" and "hello".

Never use a word relating to you or your business, and don't just pick a word from the dictionary. Use a password at least seven characters long, comprised of letters and numbers. And, don't make it up when you are drunk, as you may have difficulty remembering it later <blush>!

Packet Sniffers

If a hacker cannot easily get through your passwords he may choose to install a piece of software known as a "packet sniffer". This is located just outside your server and monitors all incoming and outgoing messages looking for strings of letters which look familiar. It may have been pre-programmed to look for strings with the appearance of passwords, or it may go straight to the throat and look for credit card details. When it finds something which makes its ears sit up it will transmit it back to the hacker so he can then analyse the interesting files in more detail.

Social Engineering

A quaint term given to the technique of calling up your access provider pretending to be you and requesting assistance on accessing part of your system. In larger companies the "social engineer" may call your help desk posing as a hassled employee who needs "a bit of help".

Virus Attacks

You will probably be familiar with the concept of viruses. The Internet versions are very much the same as the ordinary computing world "viruses". They can be present in any form of file, which comes onto your system by whatever means (though usually as an email attachment). An Internet-specific virus is known as a "Trojan horse" which may have the appearance of a useful programme for the first few months of usage and then set about destroying files on your disk. Others can be set to quietly transmit random files from your computer to an unknown recipient each time you connect, thereby doing away with the need for all that tiresome hacking.

Denial Service
This is where your Internet server is deluged under hundreds of thousands of messages rendering it incapable of functioning normally. It's kind of like high-end flaming. If your in-house network or other business computers are connected to your Internet server they could also be crippled.

Software Attack
This is possibly the worst form of security breach for a small business to handle. Unless you are a technical guru or software expert, it is highly unlikely that you will be able to patch over the holes in your operating system software which the hackers can blast their way through. However it also takes an expert to know about and locate security holes in your software. So you must really need to have something worth stealing for them to bother.

The Remedies

Password Education
Educate yourself and your staff in ways of picking new passwords. There are some software programs available which will prevent anyone from choosing an insecure or obvious password.

Packet Sniffers
Make sure that you change your passwords regularly and use this in conjunction with other security measures, like professional encryption or the use of a proxy merchant.

Social Engineering

Tell your staff not to give out any information or to discuss security with your Internet access provider. Arrange for one person to deal with your provider on these matters and ensure they use some form of identification such as the maiden name of their grandmother (so long as it was not "password").

Virus Attacks

Check everything that comes into your computer, including orders, and keep Internet downloads on a sacrificial computer or removable disk. Get the latest Anti-Virus program and keep it updated.

Denial of Service

There is very little you can do about this. You have natural protection if the rest of your business' systems are not connected to the Internet server. However, you should never get into the position where denial of service is a problem if you follow the advice given in this publication about netiquette in email and Newsgroups.

Software attacks

Use as few programs on your server as possible. And never use any software that you do not fully understand. You could turn your server into a "bastion" by installing high quality firewall software or, at a lower price, some of the free Sentinel software available on the Internet.

Chapter 15

Why Internet Businesses Fail

Rip Off

It is extremely easy to fail before you have even begun by being ripped off by unscrupulous ISPs, so-called "Internet consultants" and dodgy "web designers". With the market becoming flooded with access providers and consultants make sure that you shop around for the best deal. While the majority may be worth their salt, some are not even worth talking to. Your best defence against these operators is to learn as much as you possibly can about the Internet, and doing business on it, so you know when the wool is pulled over your eyes.

On the Internet, as anywhere, the lowest price is not always the best. Also make sure that you ask to see live examples of any consultants' or designers' work and get at least two references. Don't be afraid to ask friends and colleagues for recommendations, but beware of rave reviews in Newsgroups, which may have been put there by the company themselves!

Running Too Early

If you try to run before you can walk, you are bound to fall over. As we said earlier, keep it simple to start with and learn as you go along. Remember to plan for expansion.

Incompatibility

Closely connected to the planning for expansion comes compatibility problems. There are a lot of bits and pieces required for the successful set-up and running of an Internet presence. The Internet, contrary to some claims can never come "in a box". Your set will include a server, modem, communications links, software, firewalls, cables, cards and slots. All of them have to be mutually compatible with your current and future needs as well as the equipment used by your ISP. Unless you have a strategy for keeping everything compatible you could easily come to grief.

Trying To Do Too Much Yourself

If you are reading this book, the chances are that you cannot do all that is required to set-up an Internet presence in-house. At some stage it is wise to consult a professional or invest in the right software. Make sure you farm out some of the burden and get good advice to avoid your site becoming a damp squib.

Non-Compliance

It is impossible to swim against the tide. The Internet has been around for a long(ish) time and it is bigger than any person or organisation (witness Microsoft's struggles to gain their usual footholds). Go with the flow and do not try to change the Internet. The people on it are easily offended and are not afraid to let you, and everyone else, know about companies who ignore the rules.

Passive Shop Front

Just because you have created a site does not mean customers will come flocking to your door. You may have the best site in the world but if nobody knows it's there they cannot buy your products or use your services.

Budget time and money to be spent promoting your site as you would for a high street shop.

Ignoring Feedback

One of the good points of the interactivity afforded by the Internet is the feed back you will receive, both positive and negative. If you ignore what visitors say you are sure to be the loser.

Security Lapses

In the worst case scenario you could send out all of your stock and not receive a penny back for it, or your system could be compromised resulting in crippling downtime and/or damage to your equipment.

Ignoring the Law

The Internet may resemble the Wild West in many respects but it is still subject to the law (but of which land is still open to question). You can still be investigated for misleading advertising, libel, breach of copyright and obscenity. And do not forget that you are dealing with a global market; so watch out for those American attorneys and their outrageous compensation claims.

Wrong Products

Success may be guaranteed if you are a high tech business providing an information service. But if you deal entirely with 1lb bags of frozen peas you may have a hard time.

Glossary

Access provider

May also be referred to as an ISP (Internet Service Provider). A company which will sell you an Internet connection. It will have installed its own FTP, Gopher, Archie, news, mail and Web servers and will provide you with the necessary software to use them.

Anonymous FTP

A way of logging in to a computer and downloading files by FTP without having to identify yourself (so you don't need TCP/IP). Usually you log in as Anonymous and use your Email address as the password.

Backbone

High speed data connections which join together the big access providers. Smaller access providers need to connect to a backbone provider to gain access to the backbone. In WAN's it is the central section of the network.

Baud rate

Used mainly when referring to the speed of modems. It is the speed at which data can travel along a channel, in terms of bits per second.

Binary

Computers work by counting in ones or zeros which is known as binary.

Files stored on a computer may be either binary or ASCII. In a binary file the data is stored in seven-bit bytes; in an ASCII file data is stored in eight-bit bytes. Most systems can read ASCII files but not all can read binary files. Programs are usually binary files, while Emails are more likely to be simple ASCII files. Most Email packages do not allow the transfer of binary files.

Bits/Bytes

A bit is the smallest piece of information that a computer recognises and it's either got a value of zero or one. A byte is a group of either seven-bits or eight-bits.

Bps

Bits per second. The speed at which data can be transferred between pieces of hardware. You are most likely to come across it in relation to how fast modems work.

Browser

To download and read documents taken from the World Wide Web you need a software program called a browser. The most common are from Netscape, Mosaic and Microsoft.

Client

Software on a computer which is used to request information from the Internet. When you call up a web page you are acting as the client, and the computer you have contacted is the 'server'.

Dialup

A non-permanent connection to the Internet. A dial-up account will not use TCP/IP, so whilst connected you can not be recognised by the rest of the Internet.

Domain name

An Internet identification name that specifies where your computer can be contacted. It is written as a series of letters separated by full stops and slashes; for instance ours is **net-works.co.uk**

Download

The process of copying a file from one machine (usually the host) to another (usually yours).

Email address

An address which identifies you on the Internet and allows others to send you Email. There may be many people at a domain name, so the Email address can identify a particular person at a particular address. It is made up from your name, the symbol @ (pronounced at), and the domain name. E.g. sales@networks.co.uk.

FAQ

Frequently Asked Questions. This is a document found in most Usenet groups. It will have questions (and answers) that are most commonly asked by newcomers to the group. Read it before you post any questions in a group.

Flame

A rude message usually posted to a group or individual. Flames are considered offensive and those who do it will find themselves shunned. A flame will often incite retaliation with horrible consequences. Do not get involved in flame throwing.

Firewall

It will not protect you from flames, but it is a security measure. It prevents access to a LAN from outside networks, e.g. from the Internet. Many companies do not want others to be able to access their LAN.

Gateway

A device which translates an incoming flow of data from an outside network so that it can be used on a LAN. A gateway can be shared by many users.

Gopher

Software that can search the Internet and find information for you. You need to have a Gopher client on your machine and the host machine must have a Gopher server application. Most web browsers now have a Gopher facility. Gopher is menu driven and it will read and download documents based on your selection criteria. These documents can then be read off-line.

Home page
It has two meanings. It is the first page of a company's web site and the one you will be taken to as a default. It is also a generic term for the whole web site of a company or individual.

Host
Another computer on the Internet which allows users to connect to it. An ISP's computer is a host computer.

HTML
Hypertext mark-up language. You need to know this language to create documents to go on the World Wide Web.

HTTP
Hypertext Transfer Protocol. The way to transfer HTML documents between the client and the Web server (so others can then see them on the WWW).

Hypertext
Text on your computer screen which you click to take you to another document in the same web site or at another. Hypertext links form the basis of the World Wide Web. When creating a web site the author uses HTML to put up hypertext.

ISP
See Access Provider.

IP
Internet Protocol. This is a standard which devices on the Internet use to communicate with each other. It describes how data gets from its source to its destination.

IP address
Your Email address uniquely tells the Internet who you are. Computers need to know this but they prefer to deal in numbers so your Email address has a decimal notation known as your IP address.

ISDN
Integrated Services Digital Network. It is a network which allows you to send information in a digital form over the existing telephone lines at speeds of 128Kb. You dial up the computer you wish to access, establish a connection and send your information very quickly. ISDN lines can be installed by BT but they are more expensive to install and rent than a normal telephone line.

LAN
Local area network. A group of computers and peripherals connected together to form a network where they can talk to each other. They can vary in size from just computers in an office to hundreds across several buildings.

Modem

MOdulator DEModulator. A device which can send and receive information. It either receives information from your computer, converts it into analogue signals, and then passes them down the telephone line to another computer. Or, it takes a signal from a telephone line and converts it into a form your computer can understand. Modems operate at different speeds.

Moderator

A person who checks all the messages received by a newsgroup ensuring they are on topic. Cynics call them censors'.

Newsgroup

Internet bulletin boards where you can find out everything there is to know. There are thousands for every subject imaginable and collectively they are known as Usenet.

Packet

Data that is bundled up before being sent across a network is called a packet. It has information such as where it has come from, where it is going, what is in it and what form it is in so that the recipient computer can read it.

POP

Point of Presence. An access point set up by an Access Provider. There will be many around the country so that you can make a local priced call to a POP and then get on to the Internet.

PPP

Point to Point Protocol. It allows IP connections between two devices over both types of circuits. When you connect to your ISP you are probably using a PPP connection.

Protocol

A standard for how two devices communicate with each other, like a common language.

Router

Connects together all the networks that make up the Internet and allows the transfer of packets.

Server

A central computer, often a dedicated PC, which makes data available to the Internet.

SLIP

Serial Line Internet Protocol. Now being superseded by PPP, it is a standard which allows devices to use IP over asynchronous and synchronous links.

Spam

Internet slang for when someone indiscriminately sends the same message to various newsgroups. No one appreciates it.

TCP

Transmission Control Protocol. The major standard of all the Internet Protocols. TCP makes sure packets get from one host to another and that what they contain is understood. It takes the data to be transmitted from the application and passes it onto the IP for transmission.

Unix

An operating system running on a host machine that allows many clients to access the host's information, at the same time. Used by many of the servers on the Internet.

Upload

When you send a file or message from a computer (usually yours) to another computer (usually the host) you have uploaded your data.

WAIS

Wide Area Information Server. Allows a client to do a keyword search on several online databases at the same time.

WWW

World Wide Web. Commonly known simply as 'The Web', it has opened up the Internet to mass world-wide use. All documents on the web are hypertext-based which means they can all be linked together. You pass from one to the next by clicking on a particular word. Could soon become the definition of The Internet.

Notes

_____   _____

_____   _____

_____   _____

_____   _____

_____   _____

_____   _____

_____   _____

_____   _____

_____   _____

_____   _____

_____   _____

_____   _____

_____   _____

_____   _____

Appendix A

Etiquette on the Internet (or how to be a good net citizen - netizen!)

• **I want to join.** If you wish to be added to/removed from a mailing list contact the separate subscription address, not the list itself.

• **FAQ - Frequently Asked Questions.** If you want to participate in a group, ask the moderator or search the associated web pages for a list of FAQ's. This will bring you up to speed on the topics in the group and save you wasting yours, and others' time.

• **Check your address.** Make sure you give your address correctly and always check you are sending your message to the correct person/group.

• **Follow the thread.** Like in any conversation, you should listen in for a while before adding your bit. Before jumping into a mailing list discussion or a newsgroup read a few postings and then think about your reply first.

• **Be focused.** Make sure you tailor your contribution to a Usenet group's main area - eg. A knitting circle is not interested in the latest bug fixes for Windows.

• **Make room.** When you have finished surfing log out quickly. This will free up time for someone else. Make sure you follow the correct logout procedure rather than just unplugging your modem.

• **Keep to the point.** Verbal diarrhoea can be painful; the same can be said when surfing. Keep your messages clear and concise, focus on one point, and make your title relevant for easy searching. Use acronyms sparingly having first used the long-winded version. Use hard returns at the end of lines or your recipient may have difficulty reading your message.

• **Shouting from the rooftops.** Shouting when surfing is frowned upon, and anything in capitals is considered as shouting. If you need to emphasise a point try using icons, or asterisks.

• **Testing.** You can test out your files by posting them to alt.test or misc.test. This way others do not have to look at your test files.

• **Be a team person.** By joining in a group discussion you are becoming a team player. Address your discussion to the group, not an individual. Use Email for one-to-one chats. Ask for all replies to your question to be sent to you. Then read them and post a general reply back to the group.

• **Offensive.** There are those who will be rude on the net. An offensive file is called a flame and you should not send them, not reply to them, but basically ignore them. You can set up a global kill file so that offensive words are not passed on to you.

• **Think before you speak.** You know the problems of shooting off your mouth, so beware letting off steam from your keyboard. Think, before you speak, before you type! A message from you can be used by others for flaming, libel proceedings etc.

• **Tone.** Some people come across as much more aggressive when they write than when they speak. You can make your messages friendlier by using accepted icons.

• **Sorry.** Learners on the road can drive you mad, but you were a learner once. The same can be said on the ski slopes and on the net. Forgive people once for netiquette blunders, but not twice. Show others how to be helpful and polite and it should be reciprocated.

- **Credit where due.** If you reference anyone else's work, make sure you give it due credit. Emails and HTMLs are subject to the laws of the country for libel, breach of copyright, slander etc. So think before you slag anyone or anything off. Your Email may be taken down and used in evidence against you!

- **Privacy.** The net is a global place but Email is private and meant for you. Just like you probably would not photocopy a private letter and send it on, it is considered bad form to send on private Emails without first asking the author's permission.

- **Remind me.** Some people send and receive hundreds of Emails every day. When replying put the gist of the original request in at the start so they know what you are referring to. An informative subject heading can be enough.

- **What time is it?** Make sure your computer's clock and date/ time facilities are correct. This is appended to your message and used as reference by others.

- **Help!** You need to be able to help others to help you. If you have a problem make sure you know what to say when calling technical support. They will nearly always need you to verify who you are so have this important information easily to hand, along with the support teams' telephone number. Also you may need to be able to tell them your software serial number, customer reference number, the version of software you have etc before you get on to your specific problem.

- **Graphics.** Use small graphics images in your html documents as you do not know the speed of a recipient's modem. If you use video or voice files give some idea of their size.

- **Sign off.** Include your signature with all emails so that others can contact you.

Create Your Own Web Site

The World Wide Web is being transformed into an important business and communications tool. Millions of computer users around the globe now rely on the Web as a prime source of information and entertainment.

Once you begin to explore the wonders of the Internet, it isn't long before the first pangs of desire hit – you want your own Web site.

Whether it is to showcase your business and its products, or a compilation of information about your favourite hobby or sport, creating your own Web site is very exciting indeed. But unless you're familiar with graphics programs and HTML (the "native language" of the Web), as well as how to upload files to the Internet, creating your Web page can also be very frustrating!

£5.95/$9.95

But it doesn't have to be that way. This book, written by an Internet consultant and graphics design specialist, will help demystify the process of creating and publishing a Web site. In it you will learn:

● What free tools are available that make producing your own Web site child's play (and where to find them);
● How to create your own dazzling graphics, using a variety of free computer graphics programs;
● Who to talk to when it comes to finding a home for your Web site (If you have an Internet account, you probably already have all that you need).

The *On the Internet* series provides a detailed listing of the best sites in each category. Site addresses are given and all are reviewed in terms of content, layout and design, as well as the technical aspects such as speed of downloading, and ease of internal navigation. Finally, the authors let you know which material is free, which you need to pay for and how heavy the advertising is on each site.

Gambling on the Internet
Investment on the Internet
Sex on the Internet
Golf on the Internet

Each title
£4.95/$9.95

Find What You Want on the Internet

The sheer size of the Internet's information resources is its biggest challenge. There is no central repository of all this information, nor it is catalogued or sorted in ordered fashion.

Find What You Want on The Internet is designed to teach Internet users - from novices to veterans - how to locate information quickly and easily.

The book uses jargon-free language, combined with many illustrations, to answer such questions as:

☐ Which search techniques and Search Engines work best for your specific needs?

☐ What is the real difference between true 'search' sites and on-line directories, and how do you decide which one to use?

☐ How do the world's most powerful Search Engines really work?

☐ Are there any 'special tricks' that will help you find what you want, faster?

£5.95/$9.95

There is also a bonus chapter covering Intelligent Agents — special high-tech personal search programs that can be installed on your computer to search the Internet on your behalf, automatically.

Complete Beginner's Guide to Win 98

An easy-to-read guide to Windows 98 with simple instructions and hundreds of useful illustrations. It leads you through everything from installing Win 98 to exploring the many exciting features on offer such as the dynamic Active Desktop and revamped Explorer.

Also find out how to access the Internet using the Windows 98 Web browser, email program, newsgroup reader, Web page editor and even a Web publishing wizard. But that's not all!

It uses plain English to explain all Windows 98 has to offer; making it £5.95/$9.95 perfect for novices and experienced computer users alike: Master the new and easy-to-use Address Book... Handle multimedia, both live on the Internet and from CD-ROM and DVD. You can even turn your PC into a TV set!... Share your windows PC by creating "user profiles" which allow several different users to customise and access the desktop... Recover valuable disk space with FAT32... Discover new improved utilities to keep your PC running smoothly: Disk Defragmenter, Disk Cleanup, Maintenance Wizard, Backup, and ScanDisk... Keep Windows up-to-date using the Internet.

Book Ordering

Please order from our secure website at **www.net-works.co.uk** or complete the form below (or use a plain piece of paper) and send to:

Europe/Asia
TTL, PO Box 200, Harrogate HG1 2YR, England (or fax to 01423-526035, or email: sales@net-works.co.uk).

USA/Canada
Trafalgar Square, PO Box 257, Howe Hill Road, North Pomfret, Vermont 05053 (or fax to 802-457-1913, call toll free 800-423-4525, or email: tsquare@sover.net)

Postage and handling charge:
UK - £1 for first book, and 50p for each additional book
USA - $5 for first book, and $2 for each additional book (all shipments by UPS, please provide street address).
Elsewhere - £3 for first book, and £1.50 for each additional book via surface post (for airmail and courier rates, please fax or email for a price quote)

Book	Qty	Price

☐ I enclose payment for _____

Postage

Total:

☐ Please debit my Visa/Amex/Mastercard No:

Expiry date: ☐☐☐☐   Signature: Date:

Name: _____

Address: _____

_____

_____

Postcode/Zip: _____

Daytime Telephone: _____

startbk